Jackie Mason & Raoul Felder's Survival Guide to New York City

Also by
Jackie Mason and Raoul Felder

JACKIE MASON AND RAOUL FELDER'S GUIDE
TO NEW YORK AND LOS ANGELES RESTAURANTS

Jackie Mason & Raoul Felder's

SURVIVAL GUIDE
TO
NEW YORK CITY

Illustrations by Sean DeLonas

AVON BOOKS  NEW YORK

The recommendations and opinions expressed herein are those of the authors and do not reflect those of the publisher.

AVON BOOKS
A division of
The Hearst Corporation
1350 Avenue of the Americas
New York, New York 10019

Library of Congress Cataloging in Publication Data:

Mason, Jackie.
    [Survival guide to New York City]
    Jackie Mason & Raoul Felder's survival guide to New York City / illustrations by Sean DeLonas.—1st ed.
        p.   cm.
    Includes index.
    1. New York (N.Y.)—Guidebooks.   2. New York (N.Y.)—Humor.   I. Felder, Raoul Lionel, 1934–   .   II. Title.
F128.18.M37   1997   97-22333
917.47'10443—dc21   CIP

First Avon Books Printing: October 1997

AVON TRADEMARK REG. U.S. PAT. OFF. AND IN OTHER COUNTRIES, MARCA REGISTRADA, HECHO EN U.S.A.

Printed in the U.S.A.

FIRST EDITION

QPM   10   9   8   7   6   5   4   3   2   1

To Jyll Rosenfeld, our "poisonal" manager, who came up with the idea for this book, and who, in a short period of time, had us working day and night on her plantation to finish it. Now that we are finally done with this book, we paraphrase the immortal words of the lover Morris Resner, after he waited all night at the pharmacy as they were giving away last year's condom models: "Free at last, thank God Almighty, they are free at last."

Acknowledgments

Thanks to Larry Tompkins and Abby Notterman, who did the necessary leg- and footwork (in the proper places), provided brainpower and patience, and were constant resources of cheerful support.

Thanks also to Stephen S. Power, our editor, for his assistance and reality checks, without whom we might well have been relegated to writing our story (as opposed to only our telephone numbers) on the walls of public toilets.

And to Margaret Thatcher and Tyrone Power for all their encouragement and for letting us use their dirty jokes.

Contents

Jackie Mason & Raoul Felder's
Survival Guide to New York City

Introduction

New York is the most infuriating, frustrating, enervating, baffling, maddening, mystifying, aggravating, unfathomable, threatening, soul-crushing, wonderful city in the world and we would never want to live anywhere else.

There is no other city in the world where it is better to be rich or poor. Rich because there is nowhere else you can find so many other rich people to play with or more things and people you can buy with your money. Poor because nowhere else is there a municipal government that provides so many things to those who have not. It's partly because of the huge number of people at either extreme of the economic spectrum that New York has developed much of its dynamic tension, vibrancy, and, at times, danger.

The sense of fear that New York engenders in people is directly proportional to the distance of their birthplaces from the Big Apple. If you come from Picawa, Wisconsin, a walk down a New York street at 10 P.M. is a lesson in terror. To those lucky—or unlucky—enough to be born here, it is a case

1

of what psychologists call "habituation." Translated into a New York idiom: "If you live next to the Third Avenue El long enough, after a while you don't hear it at all." Or perhaps the indifference is genetic, derived from an *in utero* infusion of traffic fumes and the smell of newly baked bagels with the symphony of street sounds that rise up to your window like the sidewalk heat on a blistering August morning in a half-forgotten memory of childhood.

The sense of wonder that the city engenders is also directly proportional to the distance of one's birthplace from New York. In Spokane, Washington, New York glitters with all the romance and excitement of a first date with a high school football hero. To a typist in Brooklyn, it is a place to spend another day that begins by battling pressing bodies on the IRT and ends by fending off offending hands in the hallway after a movie date.

To anyone in the Big Apple for a weekend or serving a life sentence, each new day offers unknown delights and terrors. New York can enthrall you at 9 A.M., chew you up at noon, and spit you out crushed and bruised by 5 P.M. And as the city never sleeps, this process can be repeated each night. Survival for the rest of your life—or until the end of the day or until the factory whistle blows or until it's time for the next cigarette or cup of coffee—is most people's goal. As New Yorkers get more desperate, the interval in prayers gets shorter and shorter. "God get me through this day" becomes "God, get me through until lunch hour," and then becomes "God, I can't take even one more minute of this."

The regular denizens of the town have their own stratagems for survival, whether it is your brother-in-law, who has to look no further than your checkbook to impress the girl with whom he is cheating on your sister; Donald Trump, who delights in maneuvering bankers into a corner; or you, who would simply enjoy being able to get a taxi in the rain when your arms are full of packages.

From Giovanni da Verrazano sailing up the fog-shrouded East River five hundred years ago looking for a good Italian restaurant, and in the process discovering this burg, to mobsters enjoying a concrete repose entombed in the foundation of the bridge that bears the great explorer's name; from the Algonquin Indians in dirty leather shmattes sitting half naked on horse blankets in sixteen hundred something to men in two thousand dollar suits sitting on leather chairs in the lobby of the Algonquin Hotel on Forty-fourth Street to any of the people who have lived in this city at one time or another in their lives—from John D. Rockefeller to Dutch Schultz to Charles Lindbergh to Babe Ruth to Aaron Burr to P. T. Barnum to Duke Ellington to George Washington—they would all tell you they had their own private survival tips. Your problem is that you don't have these people to bother with your questions, and if you did, it would be a one-sided conversation. What you have instead is us.

We have not lived here through all the wars, riots, epidemics, famines, and floods that have afflicted New York. We were not here when the British blockaded the harbor from 1812 to 1814, when the blockade was so tight you could not buy a bottle of Perrier or a new Volkswagen in the entire city. We were not here for the great fire of 1835, when you only had to open your window if you wanted to have a barbecue for your family. We were not here for the battle of Harlem Heights on September 16, 1776, but *were* here for the Harlem riots of 1968, when instead of General George Washington we had Mayor John Lindsay leading the fight. George did better than John. With George in command, history tells us, not one television set was stolen out of a store window.

Between show business and the law business we have seen—

or been victim of—every permutation and combination of crooked, scheming, and semicrooked machinations that one person can try to employ against another to make a buck or accomplish something that would ordinarily cost more or take longer to do. Across a thousand delicatessen tables, late into the night, we have discussed, dissected, and analyzed these assaults on our own wonderfulness. Out of all these discussions and over untold amounts of half-eaten pastrami, pickles, and chopped liver we have planned and plotted and eventually come up with a comprehensive survival strategy for living in New York. This we will freely (or almost freely) share with you—along with the half-eaten pastrami, pickles, and chopped liver.

Bargains

There is something in Jewish DNA that precludes any Jew whose IQ is more than his age from paying regular retail prices. For every Jew, getting a bargain is only half the battle. The other half is to pay less than his friends.

For the last two thousand years, when two Jews meet on the train going to work and one shows the other a new watch, tie, transistor radio, or anything that costs more than forty cents, a variation of the following dialogue ensues.

"What did you pay for that?"

"Well, it lists for—"

"List? Are you crazy? Who pays list?"

"You paid too much. I bought the same thing wholesale."

"Wholesale? Forgeddit. I bought it at *cost*."

"That's nothing. I bought it at *less* than cost."

"*Less* than cost? How does he make any money selling it?"

"Easy. He sells a lot of them."

★　　★　　★

There are some places in New York offering legitimate bargains, bargains without sixty different prices and without the necessity of a consumer first having to go to Baghdad to take a crash course in bazaar marketing. The following are our favorites.

DEPARTMENT STORES

Generally speaking, if you are looking for true bargains, avoid any department store that advertises in the newspapers. How much of a bargain can the store be giving you if the high cost of their advertising has to be factored into the price of the merchandise? Also, real bargains exist usually because the store has a small quantity of a particular item remaining, and they want to get rid of it quickly. Similarly, if we are talking about a desirable item and not some reject or manufacturing mistake, a wholesaler might offer a retailer a good buy on his small amount of remaining merchandise in order to clear his shelves for next year's merchandise. Either way, the quantity of goods acquired at distressed prices by the retailer is insufficient to warrant the store owners' spending money for any sort of advertising campaign.

Likewise, avoid any store to which you remember your mother dragging you, a chocolate bar shoved into your mouth to keep you occupied. These stores are passing away from atherosclerosis. Instead, follow the hip crowd to the following.

Century 21 (22 Cortlandt Street). This is one of the great treasures of New York. Because of the diversity, quality, and discounted prices of the merchandise offered, there is virtually nothing like this store anywhere else in the country. The store sells first-quality products—including shoes, suitcases, cameras, clothes for the family, housewares, toys, lingerie, and toiletries—

all at extremely discounted prices. You can buy everything from Hanes briefs to a Ralph Lauren overcoat to a Moschino suit. Both men's and women's cutting-edge designer clothes are offered at extreme discounts. Gucci, Pucci, and Smoochie reign supreme. And if you are the kind of person who wears labels outside your clothes, this is the place for you. If you are a Jewish woman who substitutes the name of a designer for the name of an item of clothing—"This is my Versace" or "Hand me my Donna Karan" or "Pardon me for scratching, but my Armani is itching me right on my . . ."—this is certainly the place for you. Jewish women love gentile names on clothing. You would never hear a Jewish woman say, "Please hang up my Finklestein for me" or "How do you like my new Rabinowitz?"

If you are into ties (to wear, not for bondage), Century 21 has a great selection of designer ties that were originally too expensive or too wild to be sold the first time around and are now available for a small fraction of their original retail price.

The secret of the store's success is that it is owned and run hands-on by the Gindi family. The Gindis are throwbacks to the time when merchants had a sense of honor and pride in what they offered to the public. The Gindis scour the world for bargains, particularly in clothing. The clothing offered is neither rejects nor last year's styles.

Every major clothing designer produces a small percentage of garments that are held back and not sold to the major stores and boutiques when the original shipments go out. The Gindis, with an eye for the latest trends, are on the spot with ready cash. Their savings are passed directly to their customers. The profit is small, but the volume large, so everybody comes out ahead. Because of the volume of sales, the merchandise is rapidly replaced, often while the customer is contemplating a purchase. A visit a week after an earlier one may yield a completely new treasure trove of items.

Century is a place to spend several hours. The staff is young, cheerful, and they genuinely want to be of service. You get the feeling that they spend their own paychecks at the store. The store, which attracts many tourists as well as savvy New Yorkers, is often a madhouse, particularly at lunch hour, just after work, and around the holidays—but this is part of the fun. However, if you are into serious shopping, it is best to avoid these times.

Odd Job Trading (12 Cortlandt Street plus other locations). If you really want to go into sensory overload, try Odd Job. They sell closeouts on just about anything you can imagine—and on some things that will make you wonder why they were ever manufactured in the first place. But along with the junk and the products that should have been aborted, one will find quite acceptable toys, games, tools, kitchenware, bicycles, and exercise equipment. Avoid getting carried away by the bargains and ending up with something you have little use for. The suburbs are filled with people who stare at bicycles designed for midgets with one leg shorter than the other, sunglasses with built-in suntan lotion dispensers, or windshield wipers that they just *had* to buy at Odd Job because they were so cheap.

Old Navy (610 Avenue of the Americas). Old Navy isn't a sailor on Social Security, a broken-down battleship, Buick's limousine color for 1997, or even a department store in the true sense of the word. But what is sold there is cheap, and you can have fun while saving money. Old Navy is owned by the Gap, but it sells comparable merchandise for about 30 percent less than the Gap. The store also sells a hodgepodge of other items— some are cute, some usable, some are looking for a purpose, but most are attractive and trendy. There are ample offerings of shoes, clothes, all sorts of accessories—pink plastic cameras, alarm clocks, camp lights, metal dishes, orange hardcover notebooks—

all at such reasonable prices that you'll ask yourself, "I don't need this and maybe I don't even know what it is, but at these prices, how can I live without it?" Because so many people are asking this question, the stock moves very quickly. It pays to stop by regularly to check out the new merchandise to see if there is anything else new that you don't need.

When Old Navy has a sale, the prices are particularly good. You can stock up on kid's clothes for the next three years, have enough camping supplies for four years, buy enough casual trousers for seven years, and pick up two skirts—all for what you'd pay for a pair of panty hose a few blocks away at Barney's.

WOMEN'S CLOTHES

The three best places for bargain women's clothes are the discount department stores like Century 21, sample sales at manufacturer's showrooms, and upscale resale stores.

Sample Sales

Other than women who have Alzheimer's disease, watch old news on a 1950 Philco black-and-white television set, or like to sit in a car facing backward so they can see where they have been, no woman will buy last year's fashions. By next year, this year's unsold fashions are as useful to a designer as a bad case of acne in a lighted room.

The designer's method of disposing of unsold merchandise is to sell directly to the public at very low prices, as opposed to selling to a wholesaler or retailer, who sells to the general public. To preserve some shred of dignity, and to avoid the displeasure of retailers who might be selling the same fashions at much higher prices, the designers give these offerings the somewhat misleading name "sample sales." The items being sold—often only for cash (another attractive aspect to the designer)—are by no means samples. New York, the fashion capital of the world, is host to many such sales on any given day.

You will not find notices of these sales in the advertising pages of your local newspaper. There are several different ways to find out about the sales.

If you walk down Broadway or Seventh Avenue between Fortieth and Twenty-seventh streets on any weekday when it is not raining or snowing, you will be handed flyers by the many hawkers on the sidewalk. After discreetly folding and putting aside for later reference the flyers describing "Forty male dancers for your next bachelorette party or church social," turn to the ones dealing with sample sales. Decide what looks interesting and check it out. Or you can call your favorite designers' showrooms (they're listed in the telephone directory) and ask if and when they have sales. Finally, you can really feed your shopping urge by subscribing to *Fashion Update,* a monthly magazine that lists upcoming sample sales of men's, women's, and children's clothing; accessories; and bridal gowns. They even have a hot line for subscribers that announces late-breaking sales every Monday. *Fashion Update* (718-377-8873) costs $70 a year.

The problem with sample sales is the same as with other sales. It is easy to get carried away and buy things you don't want, need, or look good in because of the attractive price. If you feel such an attack coming on, ask how much it is just to buy the label and price tag. Then you can show the tag and label to your neighbor and say you bought the dress but don't like it, and you either threw it into the back of the closet or gave it away to charity. This way, at a tenth of the cost to you, she will eat her heart out just as much. Also, don't buy a gift at a sample sale and give it to your friend in a Bendel's box. If she tries to exchange it, you'll be very embarrassed.

Resale Stores

Now you can look like a million dollars on someone else's million. The average rich gentile woman is not bothered if her friends see her at twenty different affairs wearing the same evening dress. After all, it's their country, so what do they care if they are seen wearing the same dress more than once? They do not even care if they show up at a wedding and twelve other women and the bride and the best man are all wearing the same dress. But a rich Jewish woman would sooner be caught turning a trick in a broom closet at a Jehovah's Witness's convention than be seen in the same dress twice.

The question then becomes, What does a yenta wealthy enough to change wardrobes every forty seconds do with her gently (translation, worn once or twice) worn designer clothing? She consigns it to a resale shop where you can buy it for a fraction of its original cost.

Michael's Resale Dress Shop (1041 Madison Avenue at 79th Street). This second floor store sells major-league ladies-who-lunch clothing at minor-league prices in a pleasant, personal atmosphere. As older New Yorkers may remember, Michael used to put up signs in busses that read I, MICHAEL, HAVE A REAL NEED. Presumably the need has been satisfied since the selection is vast. Michael's even has a wedding dress department. Slightly used wedding dresses? Only in New York. But maybe it makes sense. We just went to a wedding where the bride was slightly used.

Second Act Resale Children's Apparel (1046 Madison at 80th Street). This is a place where rich people sell their children's cast-off clothes. We suspect that they would probably also prefer to sell their cast-off children here. Precious little Macadamia Goldstein would not be caught dead at another affair in that black velvet Italian number with the white lace collar bought especially to wear at Grandpa Harry's ninety-fifth birthday party. This is not to mention that Grandpa Harry would not want to be caught dead at his ninety-fifth birthday party. Aside from velvet dresses bought for ninety-fifth birthday parties, Second Act is packed with children's shoes, coats, and clothing for all occasions at a fraction of their original prices. There is an added advantage in buying used children's clothing, as opposed to buying used adult clothing: you usually do not have to worry that the clothing was stripped off some cadaver prior to burial or that the original owner died of an exotic communicable disease while wearing it or that the clothes are "unlucky" since the previous owner, while wearing them, was shot at Umberto's Clam House during a gang war.

MEN'S WEAR

Gorsart Clothes (9 Murray Street). Gorsart, where the oppressed dress to impress, has been selling significantly discounted, high-quality conservative men's clothing, shoes, and accessories for nearly seventy-five years. The staff is professional, the alterations are free, and the atmosphere is refined. This store is well worth a visit to the City Hall area. While there, if it is a cold day, you can stop by and be warmed by the hot air generated during City Council debates.

LS Men's Clothing (19 West 44th Street, suite 403). LS offers downtown prices in midtown. They carry all the well-known American designers. (Of course calling American designers "well-known" is like calling a Yugo "precision Yugoslavian engineering.")

All men want to wear clothes made by European designers.

If it were the worst shmatte that fit them as if the tailor were Omar the tent maker but was designed by somebody whose first name was Pierre or Dimitri, there would be a stampede to buy the suit, if the price were right. At LS, they *do* have European designer suits, and the price *is* right, but the really big plus is their custom-made suits.

Let's face it, a ready-made suit is only first class if you have a perfect body. Since most men have bodies that look like they are hosting the annual lump convention, they should really be wearing custom-made suits. But since custom tailors in New York require you to take out a mortgage or at least to sell your wife (for this you would have to go to The Lighthouse for the blind), most men are stuck with buying suits off the rack. However at LS for $495, you can walk away with a custom-made suit. Hopefully, it will be for you and not another guy.

THRIFT SHOPS

There are three certainties in life: death, taxes, and anti-Semitism. There is not much you can do about the first and third of these items, but a great deal of time is spent on beating the second. It is one of the paradoxes of American life that the richer a person is, the more time he spends on cheating the government out of taxes. A working person usually pays a greater portion of his wages and earnings to the government in the form of taxes than does a rich person. The payment of taxes affects a working person's life and lifestyle much more than the payment of taxes affects the life and lifestyle of a rich person. Yet a working person willingly goes under the tax collector's knife with nary a whimper. A rich person constantly plots, plans, and schemes about how to cheat the government out of taxes. He will spend sixty hours and ten thousand dollars with accountants and tax lawyers, sit up all night for a month plotting and scheming, all to figure out a way to save twelve dollars on taxes. This is why rich people love thrift shops. It gives them a way, both coming and going, to save taxes.

Thrift shops are stores set up by charitable institutions to acquire and sell used merchandise. They are usually staffed by little old ladies with blue hair who have a lot of time on their hands or by younger gentile women who have a guilty conscience and would rather do this than go to church where they can't talk and smoke. If you have the nerve to ask one of these women a question about the merchandise you usually have to stand staring into space until they finish a complete debriefing with another salesperson on why last night's dinner party was so miserable.

Since these stores are run by charities, you are making a charitable donation every time you give the store used clothing or other merchandise. Previously, these stores used to give you a receipt, stating the fair market value of the goods. Now, because of new Internal Revenue rulings, the stores are only permitted to give a receipt listing the items, and the donor is supposed to estimate their fair market value. Presumably, the IRS then compares these donor-determined values with values it has established for the same items. Uniquely, the Memorial Sloan-Kettering Thrift Shop receipt lists the price at which the donation is offered for sale. This should effectively establish the value of the donation. You should save your receipts and give them to your accountant so that a proper charitable deduction can be taken on your income tax return.

When you buy merchandise at a thrift store, whatever you paid exceeding the fair market value of the goods, is also a charitable deduction.

Translated into real dollars, in a state like New York, if you make a decent living, between federal, state, and city taxes you are taxed almost fifty cents on the last dollar earned. Therefore, if you give a charity one hundred dollars, and receive a hundred-dollar deduction, you are really only giving them fifty dollars, since the government would have taken the other fifty dollars in taxes anyway. If you give the charity used clothing, which you probably would have thrown out or given to your butler (butlers always work for men who wear their size suit), and you receive a hundred-dollar fair-market-value receipt for the clothes, you have made a hundred-dollar charitable donation. Similarly, if you buy something, and your receipt from the charity indicates you paid one hundred dollars over the fair market value (which is usually negligible) for the item, you have also made a charitable donation of one hundred dollars. This allows you to reduce the income on which you would have paid taxes by one hundred dollars; in effect, putting fifty dollars in your pocket.

There is nothing like the good feeling a rich person gets when he gives to charity, especially if he can make a few bucks by doing so.

There are lots of these thrift stores, especially around the Upper East Side, and they all sell top-of-the-line clothing at incredible discounts. So shop and donate with a clear conscience at some of our favorites: Out of the Closet Thrift Shop (220 East 81st Street), Spence-Chapin Thrift Shop (1430 Third Avenue), Irvington Institute Thrift Shop (1534 Second Avenue), Memorial Sloan-Kettering Thrift Shop (1440 Third Avenue).

CAMERAS

Today there are digital cameras; cameras that work on magnetic systems; cameras that develop their own pictures; cameras that compose the picture, focus the picture, decide on speed and exposure, predict the anticipated next movement of the subject and readjust settings to provide for this; cameras that take pictures and show them on TV sets or computers; cameras that take panoramic pictures; cameras that work by voice command; and cameras that communicate with you by beeps, bleeps, and pings. Even though manufacturers are cramming more and more electronics into their products, and you the photographer have to do less and less, the cameras are still getting smaller and smaller. The downside is this: The more complex your camera is, the more likely it is to break just as you set your shot up and, miracle of miracles, the crowd on the sidewalk parts to let you take your picture. And if anything goes wrong with your camera and you are not friendly with a Japanese, you are in a lot of trouble.

This is why it is vital to have as good a warranty on the camera or any other electronic gadget as possible. When you buy cameras and electronics, remember: the better the deal, the less consumer protection you are likely to have. Ask about guarantees *before* you buy. Make sure the product has an American warranty. A warranty good only if the camera malfunctions in southern Afghanistan during the monsoon is of limited assistance since, obviously, you would not set foot out of northern Afghanistan during the monsoon.

47th Street Photo (115 West 45th Street). You can't do much better than 47th Street Photo—*if* you can figure out how to shop here. The staff ignores you, there are no prices on anything, and all the merchandise is out of reach behind counters. This is no place for an anti-Semite, since the entire staff looks like they are playing hooky from a local yeshiva. But it is a good place to shop if you know exactly the make, style, and model number of a particular piece of merchandise. This store not only sells cameras, it also has a complete stock of computers, stereo equipment, air conditioners, electric cooking gadgets, quartz watches, etc.

Willoughby's (136 West 32nd Street). If you ignore the various reincarnations of this store, it is probably the oldest photography shop in the city. It is as large as it ever was, stretching between Thirty-second and Thirty-first streets, but today it is home to a dizzying selection of everything from cameras to fax machines to video games and telephones. The salespeople are not of the religiously devout nature of those found at 47th Street Photo, but the service is equally poor. Although the discounts might not be as steep as those found in some other discount houses, the variety of the merchandise, the staff's ability to handle a prospective customer in unhurried fashion, and the central location of the store make this a good place to shop or at least to comparison shop.

B & H Photo (119 West 17th Street). It is back to religion again. The sales help here look like rejects from the same yeshiva that the sales help at 47th Street Photo attended. The difference between this store and the other photographic discount stores is that B & H caters primarily to professional photographers. A visitor to the store might well be put off by the crowds of people, particularly on a Sunday, waiting for a salesperson. Although the lines are long in this store, since most of the customers are no-nonsense professionals who know exactly what they want, things move along at a rapid pace. As befits a store dealing with professional photographers, the staff is extremely knowledgeable. The attraction of the store is the availability of first-class photographic equipment, darkroom supplies in bulk, and studio paraphernalia at extremely discounted prices.

Wall Street Camera (82 Wall Street). In New York there are West Side people, East Side people and downtown and uptown people. Everything from accents, politics, and prices change with the part of town in which a person lives. Many people would sooner cross the Mason–Dixon line than go from uptown to downtown . . . particularly just to buy a camera. If you are a downtown denizen needing a camera or related equipment, take a walk to Wall Street Camera. Their prices are great, and the staff will actually speak with you. They even offer technical support by telephone.

FLEA MARKETS

On Sundays, come rain or shine, snow or heat wave, New York becomes a city of flea markets. The only thing a flea market doesn't sell is fleas. These, they give away. Flea markets are the last resting place of yesterday's dreams and tomorrow's hopes. In New York's flea markets can be found every nonliving product ever produced for the pleasure, entertainment, or substance of life. On sale are medals, old corsets, jewelry, furniture, clothing (old, ancient, and new), paintings, subway signs, books, cameras, microscopes, electronic equipment, sunglasses, old toasters, movie posters, stuffed animals, loving cups, dishes, cosmetic supplies, silverware, toys, Russian icons, military equipment, tools, pens, and watches.

Don't expect to read your name in the newspapers next week because you bought a painting for twelve dollars and it turned out to be *Whistler's Father* worth four hundred million dollars—at least. The sellers at the flea market with the long hair, dirty fingernails, and bad skin really are experts in what they are selling. If you pick up a silver spoon and ask about it, don't be surprised to learn it is George V, made by Paul Revere's brother-in-law, Irving, in his atelier located in a bad neighborhood just outside Ipswitch on a rainy Sunday in October 1792. But you *will* be surprised at the price and the fact you will not be paying a sales tax.

Trading at the flea markets begins at 5 A.M. among the

various dealers before the general public comes on the scene. It is not unusual for the item you purchased at one o'clock to have already been traded several times that morning. Flea markets are like girlfriends: some are going to cost you lots of money; some, very little; some will be hospitable; some not so; some you can get into for free; some will charge admission; some you walk away from with a smile on your face; some you walk away from itching.

Columbus Avenue Flea Market (at 76th Street). This was the first of New York's great flea markets. Open only on Sunday, it rapidly became a New York happening. Broadway and TV stars made this a post-pancake or before-brunch stop. We once spied Catherine Denueve browsing—which is about as good as a browsing can get. Quick as a flick we raced to the stand that sold old movie pictures, bought one of le Denueve for two dollars, raced back to where our glance last left the star, found her, and asked her to autograph the photograph. She undoubtedly believed she had just encountered two people who were her biggest fans, since who else would walk around on a Sunday morning with an eight-by-ten glossy photograph of her in his pocket.

This flea market was so popular, soon after opening in a public school courtyard, that it spilled over into the basement playroom and corridors of the school itself. This market specializes in down-market new clothing at steeply reduced prices, but there are also booths that sell first-class silver, home-style baked goods, militaria, posters, and artsy-craftsy folksy jewelry. This is not a place to look for antiques unless it's a new girlfriend. For the kind of antiques that you put in a corner, hang your hat over, and don't have to take out for a Chinese meal on Sunday night, you have to go further downtown.

Sixth Avenue Flea Market (between 25th and 26th streets). On Sundays, this parking lot, on the north side of Sixth Avenue (Avenue of the Americas), was doing as much business as Yasir Arafat selling Korans at the annual B'nai Brith convention. The owner must have felt he had nothing to lose by setting up a Sunday flea market. As a bit of insurance, to make up for the loss of revenue from the six cars that would have parked there, he charged a dollar admission to the flea market. This remains the only outdoor or indoor flea market in the city that charges admission.

The market became so popular that other flea markets opened in vacant parking lots on Sixth Avenue between Twenty-fifth and Twenty-fourth streets, between Twenty-sixth and Twenty-seventh streets, and on Twenty-fifth Street between Sixth Avenue and Broadway. Two more flea markets set up business in indoor garages on Twenty-fifth Street between Sixth and Seventh avenues, and a host of antique stores on Twenty-fifth Street from Broadway to Seventh Avenue decided to remain open on Sundays. The irony is, there is now so much traffic that a parking lot has opened up to accommodate all the automobiles that come into the area, drawn mostly by the flea markets in parking lots.

The parking lot and garage markets are flea markets in the truest sense. Along with jewelry and antiques that carry price tags in the thousands, sit unashamedly garbage-can variety junk, cheek to jowl with trophies for winning second place in weight-lifting contests and first place in sailing races. If pictures, paintings, or posters are purchased, the cheapest frame maker in New York, Big Apple Art Gallery at 765 Avenue of the Americas between Twenty-fifth and Twenty-sixth streets, will often do the framing job in three hours or less.

At any flea market the opening gambit from the customer

should always be, "I have no use for this, but my daughter likes it. What's the best you'll do?"

Lower Broadway Flea Market (located at Broadway and Grand Street). This market is three years old, and originally began as a repository for sidewalk junk. It has grown both in the quality of merchandise and in its reputation among flea market aficionados. The market specializes in old tools, electronics, records, tapes, and furniture. Strangely, you must enter through a turnstile set up on the sidewalk even though no admission is charged. An added benefit of this market is that if you make a left turn you are in Little Italy and have access to the many fine food stores open on Sundays. If you keep going east, you end up on the Lower East Side and Orchard Street, New York's original flea market, 150 years old and still going strong.

Beggars

In New York if you are in need of someone to talk to at any hour of the night there is no need to look up the telephone number of your ex-wife or your psychiatrist. You needn't even call your favorite 900 number. Simply take a walk down any major Manhattan street and you will be met by a dozen people eager to talk to you, all with their palms outstretched for money. Come to think of it, this sounds more and more like your ex-wife and psychiatrist. Except the people you meet on the street are in an older and more honorable profession. They are beggars. You will be beset by emissaries from the United Negro Pastrami Fund (because tourists might not know that the pastrami is a bird indigenous to New York, in tourist areas the organization becomes the United Negro Pizza Fund); alleged victims of every pestilence and misfortune that has befallen mankind since Adam, including the bubonic plague, attacks of the vapors, and ingrown toenail epidemics; beggars with a variety of missing limbs and stolen organs; self-professed veterans of every armed conflict since the War of the Philippine Insurrection; and people with a variety of stories beginning, "I left my wife on the observation platform of the Statute of Liberty about to give birth and I need five dollars to hire a helicopter to rescue her."

There are, of course, the truly unfortunate worthy of your beneficence. We all recognize that, to some degree, the measure of our own humanity is our willingness to provide for those who cannot do so for themselves and who fall between the cracks of government's ability to care for them. To give to these people may be noble but, in the last analysis, it is a matter between yourself, your conscience, and the depth of your pocketbook. We direct our attention not to these worthwhile recipients of your charity but rather to that vast number of others out there who endeavor to effect a transfer from your pocket to theirs of as much money as possible in the shortest time by chicanery, fraud, trickery, appeals to a guilty conscience, and often physical intimidation.

Allowing you to be ravaged by the beggar bandits is no less a force than the judicial system itself. These are the folks that let rapists move into your neighborhood, worry more about a murderer's dog than his victim, and are tougher on the police than on the criminals. The courts have found that begging is a protected activity under the free speech provisions of the First Amendment. In other words, the beggars' asking you for money is their form of communicating with their fellow citizens. So if you try to stop the beggar or, as a matter of fact, even your brother-in-law when he asks you for money, you are violating his constitutional rights and are risking being sent immediately to Sing Sing. Also consider that the poor hooker who actually *offers* you something in exchange for money goes to jail, while the beggar who offers you *nothing* in exchange for the money is a constitutional hero like Patrick Henry.

The easiest way to avoid a knockdown drag-out fight with your conscience (pathetic and small though it may be) or avoid looking like a miserable cheapskate to the girl you are walking with (since she has plenty of time to learn this about you *after* she marries you) is when walking out into the street to scan the horizon half a block in each direction, to see if there is any beggar or bum on your radar screen. It is vital to see the beggar before he sees you. Given the distance, and the beggar's handicap of a phony wooden leg or dark glasses and a cane, you can probably put a large enough distance between the two of you to avoid his entreaties. However, should you be spotted by one first, you will soon be caught in what will seem like a two-for-one miracle sale at Lourdes. Beggars, panhandlers, malingerers—the sick, sore, lame, and disabled—will throw away their crutches, dark glasses, and prosthetic devices and make a beeline for you.

The simplest way to deal with beggars is to walk around with a pocket full of change, much in the manner that school kids have learned to walk around with "mugging money." If a beggar approaches you, dip into your jangling pocket, regally toss out a few nickels liberally salted with North Korean tin bonkoys or Ukrainian lead kovachniks, and write it off as an urban tax for your use of the streets. The downside of carrying a pocket full of change is that beggars will hear you coming down the street and, like Pavlov's dogs, they will begin to salivate. The alternative is to walk around with one of those coin changing devices on your belt that the streetcar motormen used to wear. But this will, of course, give you a bulge under your jacket in a most peculiar spot. So unless you intend to say you are suffering from a hernia and intend to ask the *beggar* for a handout, leave the coin changer home for when your brother-in-law asks you for a handout.

Talking about illness—that is unless you consider a hernia not an illness but rather an attractive addition to your anatomy—an effective defense against beggars is to begin coughing uncontrollably, bending over, and spewing out of your mouth various colored liquids of various consistencies. Between his concerns over getting his $150 Reeboks dirty and his fear that he will contract a disease that might really make him ill, the beggar will probably run from you quicker than Dracula from a garlic bagel.

Just as the beggar has a prepared patter, you must develop defensive retorts. Proven examples are:

"*I gave at the office.*"

"*Have your secretary call mine in the morning. We will try to work something out.*"

"*I just gave money to your associate down the street.*"

"*You want money? I was just going to ask you for some money.*"

"*Didn't I see you on Geraldo's show? Can I have your autograph?*"

"*Let's go to church together and pray for God to help you.*"

"*I'm a Nazi war criminal trying to get back to Argentina. You help me and I'll help you.*"

"*My brother-in-law would resent my giving money to beggars, and if he finds out he has threatened never to take any more money from me.*"

The point of all this is to hit the beggar when he is off guard. He is used to the usual sucker who is too guilt ridden or intimidated not to reach into his pocket. Prove to him that whatever kind of sucker you are, you are not *that* kind of sucker.

Choosing a Doctor

If you are talking about survival you are talking about living. If you are talking about living you are talking about health, since there are not many dead people who are healthy. If you are talking about health and you are Jewish, you are talking about doctors. Gentiles live to be 104, play squash, drink martinis, and never see a doctor. If a Jew is over 27 he has a meaningful relationship and rents a room with his doctor. Jews know more about doctors than anybody else in the world. If you speak to one Jew, he will tell you he has the best doctor—that his doctor is so big you have to wait seven months for an appointment. Ask another and he will tell you his doctor is so big you have to wait fourteen years for an appointment and he has never even *seen* the doctor.

Then the Jews start speaking about how important their doctors are. One will say, "My doctor's the head of the heart department." The next one will say, "My doctor's the head of Mount Sinai." The next one will say, "My doctor is the head of Mount Rushmore." The fourth one will say, "My doctor is head of all the hospitals in the city. He is so big that nobody has even heard his name in years."

Jews also love sickness. They love to get together and compare illnesses. A gentile will have thirty-four stitches in his stomach and go to work the next day. If a Jew cuts his finger, he walks around the room giving instructions—who should blow on it, who gets the antiseptic, who gets the bandages, and who calls the doctor.

By virtue of careful hit–and–miss processes, we have developed a list of doctors that anyone who wants to survive in New York should have. Unfortunately, particularly in big cities like New York, doctors often advance in their profession by playing golf with the right people. Also, as far as the public is concerned, if a doctor has gray hair and he doesn't hurt you when he takes blood, he is a good doctor. We concentrate on all bald-headed doctors who hurt you when they take blood but are still great doctors.

There are several problems in trying to get to see the "right" doctor for your particular sickness. Everybody has medical insurance or is a member of some kind of medical coverage plan. The doctor you may want to see may not be on your plan. Even if a particular specialist *is* on your plan you cannot just go and see him and expect the plan to pay his bill.

First you have to make an appointment with your regular ordinary doctor assigned to you under your plan. *He* has to decide if you need a specialist before you can go to see one, and after he decides you need one, he will recommend a particular one to you. After waiting two weeks for an appointment with your regular doctor, since he does not want to lose a customer to another doctor, you will have a tough time convincing him that you, in fact, need a specialist.

"What, I'm not good enough for you? You need a fancy specialist? Here, take this prescription first and see if it works.

If it doesn't, come back to me in two weeks and we will see if you really do need a specialist."

The prescription is, of course, illegible to everyone but the pharmacist. He understands what it actually says, which is: "I got my money, now you get yours."

When you come back to the doctor two weeks later, and it is apparent that you do need a specialist, the doctor will send you to the specialist *he* wants you to see, not the one *you* want to go to, even if your choice of specialist is also a member of the same plan or panel of doctors. The reasons are simple: he would rather choose a doctor he knows and with whom he is friendly because he gets referrals from that specialist. It is a mutual back-scratching operation, an operation they care more about than the operation you may need. Also, if the first doctor botched up, gave you the wrong medicine or treatment, or made the wrong diagnosis—telling you that you had a pimple when you actually had pancreatitis—the specialist the first doctor sends you to is less likely to rat on him and more likely to cover up for him than a stranger of your choice.

By the time you get to a specialist under the present system, you will either have passed away or the disease will have cured itself.

To understand the dynamics of choosing a doctor, one has to understand the politics of medicine and how recent events— really tragedies—have had an impact on one's choice of a doctor.

All medical care, treatment, and even annual checkups have one goal in mind: to keep you out of a hospital. All of us, eventually, are going to be sick enough at one point in our lives to end up in a hospital. Since only the really sick are in hospitals, the care and treatment we get at a hospital may well determine if we survive or not. All previous medical care is but a prelude to this. Naturally, along with all the other things that make a great hospital is the plant, treatment facilities, and medical school affiliation. But the most important factor is still the quality of the doctors.

The two leading hospitals in the New York area are the Columbia Presbyterian Medical Center, affiliated with the Columbia University College of Physicians and Surgeons, and New York Hospital-Cornell Medical Center, affiliated with Cornell University Medical School.

Columbia's problem was that it was located on Fort Washington Avenue, near Columbia University. The trouble with being located so far uptown is that on a busy day, given the realities of traffic, a person could start the trip to the hospital suffering from one disease, recover, catch a different disease, and pass away en route while the doctors are experimenting with a new cure.

The people who run Columbia came up with an answer. In order to attract the downtown crowd—or at least those members of the crowd that did not feel like they were prepared to make long-range travel plans every time they wanted to visit their doctor (not to mention avoid drive-by shootings)—Columbia would buy the old Le Roy Hospital on East Sixty-first Street, best remembered as a drying-out spot for the town's richest drunks (with an occasional face-lift thrown in here and there); buy the best equipment, including CAT scan and MRI devices; and staff it with the brightest and best of their younger doctors. Since medicine has now become so highly specialized, this would also give the patient walk-in access, under one roof, to multiple specialists. Therefore, if a patient goes to a Park Avenue specialist complaining of a pain in his right hand and tells the doctor he also has a pain in his left hand, now he doesn't have to be subjected to, "Oh, a pain in your left hand? I will have to refer you to Dr. Schwartz on Seventy-sixth Street. He specializes in left hands up to the wrists. I only do right hands up to the wrist. If the pain in the left hand has gone into your wrist, then you better also make an appointment with Dr. Kaplan on Central Park South. He does left wrists, but if the left wrist caught it from the right wrist, then you have to go to Dr. Epstein on Sutton Place who specializes in traveling wrist pain, but only if it went from right wrist to left. If it traveled the other way, then you have to see Dr. Goldstein on Madison Avenue."

The facility flourished at a respectable rate of growth. Then it benefitted from the bad publicity surrounding an unanticipated and unwanted series of events at New York Hospital. Andy Warhol went into the hospital for a gallbladder operation, so routine and simple that any surgeon could do it without even putting on rubber gloves. Instead of waking up without a gallbladder, Warhol woke up dead. Libby Zion, eighteen-year-old daughter of brilliant columnist Sidney Zion, went into the emergency room suffering from the flu. Several hours later, tragically, she was dead. This time somebody died whose family had an articulate and loud public voice. Now when these stories became public knowledge, no Jew with more than fifty dollars in the bank would take his sickness here. As a result of New York Hospital's (not to mention the patients') misfortunes, the Columbia facility prospered and, in fact, moved to a larger building at 16 East Sixtieth Street.

Because of the complexity, variety, and subjectivity involved in evaluating the different medical options, and in particular the individual doctors available in New York, we instead have chosen to recommend the Columbia facility on Sixtieth Street, with its staff of young and able specialists, all under one roof.

We particularly recommend Dr. Benjamin Lewis, as both a cardiologist and internist. He is a pioneer in the echo stress cardiogram, a completely noninvasive heart-testing procedure that compares favorably with all these tests requiring you to get injections that make you glow in the dark. He has gadgets and tchotchkes to diagnose and treat every possible heart ache you can get except the ones you get when you are jilted by a blond showgirl. His staff is homey and have wonderful listening ears, treating each patient with the warmth you would give to a rich relative who is about to make a will and has just stopped by for a cup of coffee.

Dr. Lewis Schneider, gastroenterologist, makes a specialty of inserting long snakelike tubes into every available orifice for diagnoses and treatments. His expertise allows the procedures to be over in the shortest possible time . . . not a small blessing. He and his friendly and sensitive staff make the unendurable, if not pleasant, at least tolerable. Of course, if you are among those who do recreationally what Dr. Schneider does to you professionally, you will have a ball.

If your plumbing is the problem or if you are over the age of fifty and need a checkup, urologist Dr. Lloyd Benson is the man for you. He is the fastest man with a quip or a finger in the building.

The dermatology department at the Columbia East Side facility, under Doctors Robert Bickers and Robert Walther, is the best in the city. Appointment and waiting times are very short, as there are at least ten nurses and medical people in attendance at all times with as many as half a dozen board-certified dermatologists present at any one time. The equipment is extensive and state-of-the-art. There are three light booths and special baths for patients with psoriasis, as well as laser and surgical facilities. This is the perfect place to send your skin diseases.

There are, of course, standout individual doctors who are not affiliated with the Columbia facility. Other outstanding individual physicians, listed by specialty, about whom we can speak highly follow.

Ophthalmology: Dr. Anne Marie Mc Veigh. Dr. Mc Veigh is a fossil. Doctors like her have gone the way of the nickel cigar and a two-cent glass of seltzer. She will spend as long as she feels necessary with a patient, often as much as an hour. Money seems to be of little or no interest to her (this may be a genetic problem with her). Skilled and dedicated, she is probably the last ophthalmologist in New York who will make a house call. She is too good and decent to be real. At the very least, she should either be preserved in formaldehyde or made a saint.

Ear, Nose, and Throat: Dr. Andrew Blitzer. All Jewish men, from the first time their mothers took them to a doctor, have a problem with either tonsils or adenoids. If they have had them taken out, then it's their sinuses or at the very least, if it concerns their noses, they have a "condition." Dr. Blitzer takes this sort of thing very seriously and painstakingly tries to eliminate each possible cause, rather than, as is the usual custom, simply prescribing the medicine *du jour*. He is also one of the leading experimenters in the use of highly diluted botulism solutions for the eradication of frown lines. He assures us, in the strengths he administers the solution, it will only get rid of the frown, and not the rest of your body.

Plastic Surgery: Dr. Daniel Baker. Dr. Baker is the present king of plastic surgeons. As with any king, you will have to wait a long time for an audience. There is presently a ten- to fourteen-month waiting list for operations, and at least that long a wait for an appointment. It is well worth the wait to have Dr. Baker's magic fingers work on you. Even if you are ready to plunk down hard cash he will refuse to operate on you if he feels you do not need it or your expectations are unrealistic. Notwithstanding his ministrations to the rich and famous, he has devoted hundreds of hours operating without charge, both here and in Vietnam, on otherwise hopeless cases. Even if you don't need plastic surgery, he is such a good person, you should send him a couple of dollars.

Baldness: Dr. Joel Kassimir and Dr. Jerome Shupack. One does it from the outside in, the other from the inside out. Dr. Kassimir transplants hair, and Dr. Shupack of NYU was a pioneer in minoxidil research.

The original hair transplant experiments involved transplanting hair from a dog to a man. It seemed to work, but the only drawback was that every time the recipient passed a hydrant, he had an urge to lift his leg up and urinate. But we digress.

Pediatrics: Dr. Daniel Notterman and Dr. Harris Burstin. Dr. Notterman heads the Pediatric Critical Care Unit at New York Hospital. If your boss is giving a dinner party that if you don't attend you will lose your job, or if you were just given a pair of Knicks tickets and have no place to leave your children, then this is a critical care emergency. You should call Dr. Notterman so you can park your children with him. If, on the other hand, the affair you are going to is not *that* important, or the girl you have the date with is *not* that much of a knockout, then Dr. Burstin of NYU, who has the best waiting room full of toys, is the place to dump the kids.

Psychiatry: No recommendations. Anybody who wants to go to a psychiatrist should have his head examined.

Body Parts Specialists. Foot or ankle: Dr. Jonathan Deland, Hospital for Special Surgery.

Hands: Dr. Keith Raskin, New York University Medical Center.

Hips: Dr. Eduardo Salvati, Hospital for Special Surgery.

Knee: Dr. John Insall, Beth Israel Medical Center.

Further Specialties. Addiction: Dr. Anne Geller, St. Luke's-Roosevelt Hospital Center.

Allergy and immunology: Dr. Ellen Buchbinder, Mount Sinai Medical Center.

Dementia: Dr. Daniel Sciarra, Columbia Presbyterian Medical Center.

Epilepsy: Dr. Joel Cohen, Montefiore Medical Center; Dr. Timothy Pedley, Columbia Presbyterian Medical Center.

Geriatric medicine: Dr. Diane Meier, Mount Sinai Medical Center.

Headache: Dr. Carolyn Barley Britton, Columbia Presbyterian Medical Center.

Infertility: Dr. Zev Rosenwaks, New York Hospital. Note: If you are an anti-Semite and have a fertility problem, you are in a lot of trouble, since almost all of the fertility specialists in New York are Israelis.

Obesity: Dr. Louis Aronne, New York Hospital.

Obstetrics & gynecology: Dr. Manfred Epstein, New York University Medical Center.

Orthopedic sports medicine: Dr. Barton Nisonson, Lenox Hill Hospital.

Pain management: Dr. Emile M. Hiesiger, New York University Medical Center.

Parkinson's disease: Dr. Govindian Gopinathan, New York University Medical Center.

Stroke: Dr. John Caronna, New York Hospital.

Tattoo removals: Dr. Roy Geronemus (uses laser surgery).

Construction and Contractors

As soon as a Jew makes some money he has to develop a meaningful relationship with a construction man. There hardly exists a Jewish person who can do anything with his hands. The simple fact is that Jews were raised never to do anything with their hands except to pick up a phone to call a gentile to do the work. If a Jewish car breaks down, that's it! The man and his wife stare at it for twenty minutes, then the wife says, "It stopped." The husband says, "It's under the hood." The husband then asks a passing gentile where the hood is. When he finds out, it takes him three hours to figure out how to open it. After he finally understands how to open it and is about to do it, the wife screams, "Watch out, you'll hurt yourself." When at last he finally has the hood open, he marvels about how busy it is in there and hails a cab to take him and his wife to a car dealer to purchase a new automobile while they discuss whom they can sue.

This fundamental difference between Jews and gentiles is even more acute when a home is involved. A gentile home is one large workshop; whereas a Jewish home is a museum with everything covered in plastic. A visitor who sits on a chair not covered in plastic or puts a drink down without something under it on a table, risks getting stabbed right in the heart. When you enter a gentile home, you hear hammers banging, and nails and screwdrivers are flying around the room. The gentiles are fixing everything—building, rebuilding, and changing. The living room was once a kitchen, the toilet was once a chair, the Ping-Pong table was once a furnace, and the second floor was once a chimney. As you are sitting there they are chopping up the floor around you to put up a bigger house. Fixing something is like an orgasm to a gentile.

A Jew fixes nothing! He either imports and exports or exports and imports. Everything is coming and going. The house is one big shipping department. Jews are always telling you what's coming or what is about to come. A Jewish home is really a post office.

The great pride in a Jewish house is a designer toilet. The great pride in a gentile house is the designer screwdriver. While a Jew shows you the latest fabric from Clarence House, a gentile is showing you the latest hammer and wrench he just received mail order from Bob Vila. Gentiles and Bob Vila are a set. Ask a Jew who Bob Vila is and he will say, "I saw him when he and his trio were the opening act for Tony Bennett twenty years ago." Ask a gentile that question, and he will take you to his basement and show you the Bob Vila Memorial Lounge.

This is all not to suggest that Jews don't have screwdrivers in their homes. They do—but they are called butter knives. You can always tell which butter knife is the screwdriver since its point is *zerhaggert*. You can also always tell when a Jew has put a screw in the wall, since there is a little cream cheese around the hole.

Eventually, every Jew who owns a house or an apartment needs some major repair or renovation. At this point, a contractor enters the scene. If you believe in "truth in labeling," the contractor should come to see you with a mask and a gun.

There are several basic realities that you must accept in dealing with contractors.

PENALTY CLAUSES

Contractors all lie about the length of time it will take to do the job. If somebody were to tell me I had six months to live, I hope it would be a contractor. I would then be guaranteed a minimum of another thirty-five years of life. One must accept that it is in the nature of the contractor to lie. There are obviously unpredictable delays in the course of a job—problems with availability and delivery of materials, weather, labor problems, illness, etc. Equally obvious is the fact that the bigger and longer the job, the greater the possibility for delays. However, the real problem usually is that the contractor, in the course of your job, is hired for another job. Since he has received a down payment on that job, with an owner who wants him to begin the new job, the contractor pulls men off your job to begin the new one. This can happen several or more times in the course of a job.

To avoid this happening, before you hire the contractor, insist on a penalty clause in the contract. If the contractor says the job will take thirty days say, "All right, but I want a clause that says for every day over forty-five days that the job is not completed, two hundred and fifty dollars comes off the price." At this point in time—and probably for the last time—in your relationship with the contractor, you are in the driver's seat.

The contractor would probably sign a laundry ticket if you put it in front of him.

HIRING A LAWYER

It is remarkable that perfectly sensible people who would hire a lawyer before they negotiate a tip for the men's room attendant would not hesitate to negotiate and approve a contractor's agreement without the benefit of a lawyer. Your contractor will be happy if you do not hire a lawyer to oversee the contract. This alone should be a tip-off that you should have a lawyer.

PREPARATION OF CONTRACT

If you have a lawyer, or are foolish enough to oversee the contract yourself without a lawyer, make sure your side prepares the contract, or at least its first draft. Virtually everybody leaves it to the contractor to submit the initial agreement. A contractor, being the congenital liar that he is, will put clauses in the agreement that protect him and often do not even reflect the understanding of the parties. A miraculous thing happens when something is presented already printed up. It is almost as if it is carved in stone, and thus it becomes very difficult to change. If you are, in fact, able to change parts of it, you are still dancing to variations of the contractor's music.

"EXTRAS"

When you start asking for additional things not in the contract, that is when the contractor and his wife throw a party for all their friends. In talking about additional items to the contract, some men, and most women, get carried away in giving instructions to contractors. They think they are J. P. Morgan with a cigar in their mouth, or at least Cecil B. DeMille directing a scene in a movie. When you start telling a contractor that you would like an extra cabinet in the kitchen or a different shower head or sink, the costs start piling up and economically the situation gets out of control. Let Donald Trump be Donald Trump; you are better off not adding anything to the original contract. Many people succumb to the feeling that if they don't make the additional alterations or repairs right now, rather than putting them off, they will never do it. It pays to wait for the Saturday night dance since Saturday always comes around. In other words, wait to put on any additions.

PURCHASES

There should be a very clear understanding about purchases of separate consumer items. If the contractor buys an item, he charges you the list price while he purchases it at a dealer's discount, or 20 to 30 percent less. If you know in advance whether you want any additions—for instance, a particular microwave oven or stereo set—and you have a friend who can get it for you at cost or, if you are really lucky, below cost, you should preserve the right to purchase it yourself. It is best to put everything concerning purchases in the contract itself.

VISIT THE JOB

It is very important to make frequent visits to the job site. This is something that cannot be delegated. A fixture that looks perfect in a catalogue may look awful in your house. Furthermore, as for the progress being made on the job, you can believe the reports of the average contractor as much as you can believe Muammar Qaddafi. The only difference is that your contractor probably only wears a dress at night, whereas Qaddafi wears one all day long.

DRY RUN

Take a shakedown voyage in your new or altered home before you pay the contractor. In other words, spend a night in the new place. You may find that areas of the house are not properly illuminated, switches are inaccessible, lighting is too harsh or too dim, water flow in the shower is insufficient, etc. The only way you can know these things is to actually stay overnight in the house or apartment. After doing this, if you have an argument with a contractor about any condition, you are in a position to say that he doesn't know what he is talking about since *he* has not slept there, unless, of course, he is overfriendly with your wife.

In short, dealing with a contractor is like hiring a hooker: it is better if you never have to do it. But if you do, hold on to your wallet, make sure you are in the driver's seat, and believe only about half of what they tell you.

Decorators

Sooner or later every woman (sooner if the woman is Jewish) whose husband makes four dollars a year more than her best friend's husband decides she has to change the plastic covers on the living room sofa and, of greater significance, has to hire a decorator.

Just like the fact that every man believes he is a lover, every yenta believes she is a decorator. Since you don't need a license or have to pass any test or even not be color-blind to call yourself a decorator, all any woman has to do to call herself a decorator is to purchase a resale number from New York State and print up cards with the title Decorator. If she really gets carried away with herself, her card reads Interior Designer.

The resale number is a vital component of the decorating business, since it enables the decorator to avoid paying sales tax when she purchases an item from another dealer or a wholesaler. The theory is that, since the decorator is a legitimate business person, she will charge the ultimate consumer of the product, the person she sells to, the sales tax. Otherwise the state would be collecting the same sales tax twice. In most cases, however, the decorator has two customers—herself and her sister-in-law—and the purchase of the resale number is nothing more than a gimmick to avoid paying sales tax. Such practices are, of course, strictly against the law, but because there are more yentas and sisters-in-law than tax collectors, this crime usually goes unpunished. But every now and then, the state cracks down. Therefore, unless a woman would like to accept the possibility that the bracelets her neighbors might see her leaving the house with were supplied by the NYPD and not her husband or her Italian construction boss lover, this is not a practice to be followed, especially since the money saved is peanuts and deductible on the federal tax return.

The fancy business card gets decorators into the wholesale houses, either by themselves or with their customers. In New York there are whole buildings devoted to selling furniture and tchotchkes to decorators.

Being a decorator is the only business in the world where you don't need a store, merchandise, or even any ability in your field. All you need is a business card and a yenta looking for another yenta to hire. That the yenta being hired doesn't know any more about decorating than the one who hires her is not important. The important thing to the employer is that she is able to mention "my decorator" around the mahjong table. It is quite true that there is an American Society of Interior Designers that requires decorators to pass an examination and agree to a code of ethics before they can put ASID after their names. However, there never was a Jewish housewife in the history of the world who did not hire a decorator because she did not have these initials after her name. We know a decorator who would not know purple from pickles and yet had, on her stationery after her name, the initials ASID. When questioned, she

said that we should look closely. The *D* is really an *O,* with the
initials reading ASIO. Translation: "any shmuck is overcharged."

There are fewer and fewer professional decorators in business
each year since, as with sex, with all the amateurs available, the
professionals can't make a living.

An honest decorator, traditionally, has been as hard to find
as a gigolo in an impotency clinic. The problem is that decorators usually function as furniture salesmen, charging any markup
they see fit to a customer who is not in a position to question
the price. Worse yet, decorators are in positions of trust, having
been hired by the customer to protect the customer from people
like themselves.

One variation of the payment arrangement with a decorator
is for the decorator to charge the client list price for every item
the decorator purchases, keeping the difference between the discount price and list. The problem is that the decorator, who
often enjoys a cozy relationship with the dealer, is able to ask
the dealer to increase the list price, thereby increasing the
decorator's profit. To make matters even more unfair for the
customer, often the items the decorator purchases are one-of-
a-kind items, so that the customer has no way of determining
what the fair list price should be.

Another decorators' billing method is a fixed fee, based on
a flat fee, which in turn is based on the overall budget. In this
case, the decorator passes on to the client only the alleged net
cost the decorator pays for items purchased. Here, too, there is
the possibility of overstating the list prices. A variation of this
method is a fixed fee that is a precise percentage of the moneys
spent for the job, computed on the decorator's net cost. Yet
another method is simply hourly billing, anywhere from $150
to $400 an hour. It should be borne in mind that the decorator
will charge for her time for everything from shopping to

chatting. And if you have a decorator who talks slowly you can be in an awful lot of trouble.

Marrianne Bihari of Bihari Interiors, one of the few honest decorators with good taste that we know, points out that customers can be particularly selective these days. Retail stores are no longer devoid of high-style merchandise, and stores offer free design consulting services to customers. She says she welcomes clients who question cost and is happy to show them her original invoices and mostly tries to steer them away from items overpriced or not in their budgets. But decorators with this philosophy are few and far between.

Our best advice: if you cannot do it yourself, set a minimum budget and use the same common sense to pick a decorator that you would use to pick a wife or husband. Since only one third of marriages end in divorce, you should have a sixty-six and two thirds chance of finding a good decorator.

Finding an Apartment

If you work in New York there is absolutely no problem in finding an inexpensive, spacious apartment in a nice neighborhood. However, the morning commute from Anchorage might leave you somewhat the worse for wear, and, of course, there is the problem of where you will leave your snowshoes once you get to the office.

If you want to find an apartment in the New York area where you don't need a Sherman tank in order to walk the dog; where you don't have to share a combination refrigerator, sink, and toilet located behind the boiler in the basement with four hundred other tenants; where you don't have to board the Concord to get to work every morning; and the rent is less than $280,000 a year, you have two choices. The first is to pray a lot. The second is to read the following very carefully.

Walking into Rick's Café in Casablanca with hundred dollar bills coming out of every orifice, looking for a letter of transit to Canarsie, you would have less chance of being a victim of a scam than you would looking for an apartment to rent in New

York. Since apartments are not susceptible to being wrapped up and put in a brown paper bag to take home with you, it is particularly easy for a scam artist to sell you the *idea* that you have just purchased the right to an apartment lease.

The first rule of apartment hunting is "avoid scams." Unfortunately this is like saying "avoid pastrami" as you are going into a delicatessen. Sadly, when you are looking for an apartment, unscrupulous and bogus individuals are as prevalent as hookers on a summer evening on Ninth Avenue. They both end up doing the same thing to you, except with them, as opposed to the ladies whose businesses are located on Ninth Avenue, you don't have to take your clothes off. Consider the following examples.

SCAMS

The Application Fee Scam

In this scam, a vacant apartment will be advertised and shown with no intention of actually renting it. The real intention is to use a vacant apartment as bait for a period of time before it is actually rented. The unsuspecting sucker sees an advertisement for an "open house" on an apartment that seems to be a great deal. It *is* a great deal. However, the great deal is for the broker, not the sucker. After the sucker looks over the terrific apartment, he is asked to complete an application and pay a nonrefundable application fee and is told if he is found acceptable for the apartment he will receive a call. In the real world he has as much chance of hearing from the "broker" as he does of hearing from the New York State Lottery Commission or exchanging vital body fluids with Demi Moore. The sucker simply assumes he didn't get the apartment. But where has his money really gone, besides out of his wallet?

Sometimes, the application fee is inflated. The broker then pockets the difference between his actual costs and what he has been paid. A standard credit check runs about thirty-five dollars. Add a little for administrative costs. If the sucker pays more than fifty dollars, he has been had. The bottom line: if the nonrefundable application fee sounds high, don't apply. To add insult to injury, if there is a real apartment that eventually will be rented to someone and some sort of credit check *is* actually done and the sucker is not a member of some persecuted minority group like circumcised midgets, the broker has done nothing illegal.

In other cases, the broker isn't really a broker at all. He shows an empty apartment in a building his brother-in-law owns, pockets the fee, then disappears after sharing his loot with his brother-in-law who will swear he has never seen the man before. To prevent your money ending up in some brother-in-law's pocket—other than your own brother-in-law's, where it usually has its final destination—always make sure you are dealing with a reputable broker. You can do this by asking for a business card and calling the phone number. It will be immediately apparent whether it is the brother-in-law answering or if you are calling a real working brokerage office. Also, go back the next day and see if the apartment is still available. If it is not, stop payment on your check.

The Disappearing Apartment Scam

When looking for an apartment there are worse things that can happen to you than losing a few dollars in a phony application fee or having your brother-in-law show up as you are moving in accompanied by his wife, four gerbils, seven goldfish, and three ugly children with hammers in their hands just as your wife informs you that she forgot to tell you she invited them to stay at the new apartment while their home was being repaired because of the hammer damage done to it by the three ugly children.

You are shown an apartment that you fall in love with and decide this is the place to raise your own ugly children. Your application is accepted; you happily pay the landlord a month's rent and a security deposit. The key is placed in your trembling, eager hand and you are told the apartment will be available the first of next month. Unfortunately, the departing tenant is so upset and angry at having to give up this gem of an apartment that he is uncooperative and will not let anybody into the apartment until his lease has expired.

When you finally arrive on move-in day with your wife, your own ugly children, and all your worldly belongings, you find that the key doesn't fit the lock and there is someone else, with their own ugly children, already living in the apartment. Your money is gone and so is the "landlord."

A good con artist can pull this off. All he needs is the key to a vacant apartment and fifty dollars to pay off the doorman (if there is one). Usually the scam involves an apartment in a small building without a doorman or live-in superintendent or a building where the doorman or superintendent is working together with the con artist.

You can avoid the drama in the hallway by making sure the person who rented you the apartment, usually a managing agent, is really employed by the management company. You should also confirm that the management company employing the agent really handles the building into which you are moving. The information concerning the management of the building, including telephone numbers, is, by law, on a card posted inside the entrance to the building. This card will give you the landlord's and/or the management company's name and telephone number. Make sure this is the same information you have previously been given. A telephone call will affirm or disaffirm any suspicious information.

Finally, if you are subletting an apartment, ask for a copy of the original lease. Then call the owner listed on the lease to make sure it is still in effect and that no one is contesting its validity in a lawsuit. The owner will undoubtedly ask you why you want the information. Make up any credible story. Tell him you are with the Polish secret police and you are doing a background investigation on the tenant who is rumored to be the last living descendant of King Ladislaw the Cleaver and the government of Poland is considering gold-plating the apartment but only if the tenant's genealogy can be established. If not, the standard washable wallpaper is all they will go for. Whatever you do, do not tell the owner you are thinking of subletting the apartment. Owners, capitalist pigs that they are, if they hear about a sublet *before* it occurs, will think up some way to make a profit on the deal. After you speak to the owner and establish that the lease is still in effect, then read it over very carefully to make sure the tenant offering to rent it to you actually has the right to sublet. Sometimes the landlord has the right to approve or disapprove any sublet. Even if the lease gives the landlord an unqualified right of approval, the law may not permit him to exercise this important tenant right unreasonably. Often the lease only allows the tenant to make a modest profit on a sublet, the balance of the profit going to the landlord. If this is the case, push extra hard to make a terrific deal. Since any additional profit will be going to the landlord, the tenant you would be renting from will be less than zealous in negotiating with you if the only thing he will be accomplishing is to make his landlord richer.

Bait and Switch

This is a classic scam found in the purchase of any consumer item from live chickens to television sets. It is also a common ploy of Jewish mothers. They will meet a woman in a beauty shop whose son is a doctor. "Have I got a girl for your son!" A girl will be described who is a cross between Madame Curie and Demi Moore. When the hapless doctor finally meets the girl for a date, he is presented with a toothless wretch whose breath could be used as a secret weapon against Saddam Hussein. Apartment renting is not exempt from this kind of scam.

A real estate broker advertises a great-sounding, no-fee apartment. When you meet the broker—just *your* luck, you, who have suffered every cruel cut of fate from being cursed with a wife, who came as a package with a live-in brother-in-law in the world-class-eater category, to chronic ingrown toenails on all your counting toes—you now are told that the magical apartment you raced across town to acquire, sight unseen, has just been rented. But wait, you are told another more expensive, perhaps a bit less desirable apartment is available—of course . . . for a fee. You now have your first opportunity to make your own good luck. Run, don't walk, from that real estate broker. Better yet, call your brother-in-law and tell him, "Boy, have I got a great apartment for you!"

HOW DO YOU FIND OUT ABOUT APARTMENTS?

Talk to People

The modern version of the jungle drums, word of mouth, is a tried-and-true means of finding almost anything in New York, including an apartment. Ask your relatives. Ask friends and colleagues. Call the housing office at your alma mater even if it is a reform school. Go to the UN and hospitals in the neighborhood in which you are interested and see if there is anything on their bulletin boards worth pursuing. Ask to see the human resources director at the biggest company in your neighborhood of choice and inquire if you can put a notice on the bulletin board describing the kind of apartment you want. The answer will always be yes, so come prepared with an index card, ready for posting, describing your needs.

Walk around a neighborhood in which you would like to live and ask doormen about vacancies (be prepared to tip for answers). If you are prepared to speculate and are in love with a particular building, give the doorman ten dollars and tell him, "There's more where this came from," if he notifies you the *instant* he hears an apartment will be available. Often, because of the gossip telegraph in an apartment house, the doorman will learn of an impending vacancy before the landlord.

Ask the neighborhood mailman. Check with the dry cleaner, the deli, the barbershop, learn Korean and ask at the local nail salon where neighborhood gossip is a staple along with bad manicures. Talk to bartenders, waitresses, and the guy you see walking his dog at eight every morning. You get the idea. Someone will know someone who's moving to Bali and needs to find a renter in the next half hour.

Read the Papers

The Sunday *New York Times* is available on Saturday night, and Wednesday's *Village Voice* is sold outside the Astor Place subway station on Tuesday night. There will be a crowd of people huddled around the newsstand waiting for the papers to arrive. If you don't find an apartment, at least you may get a date or, if you are lucky, a roommate. Once you find a likely apartment listed in the paper, start making calls immediately. If you wait until the next day, you may find you are only one banana in a very big bunch. When working through newspapers, don't forget the large number of neighborhood papers and newsletters. These papers, which all have real estate sections, can be picked up in the lobbies of large apartment houses and in plastic boxes on street corners. They can also be obtained at the publishers' offices, which are listed in the papers themselves and also in the telephone directory. Often one publisher will own several neighborhood newspapers, so that you might walk away with a handful of different papers as a result of one visit. Best of all, the papers are usually free.

Check Bulletin Boards

Aside from hospital bulletin boards, visit local graduate schools and universities, as they generally allow people to post notices involving living quarters. You should also look for bulletin boards around the neighborhood. They are often found in Laundromats, gyms, and health food stores. These sources virtually guarantee you will be renting an apartment from a healthy athlete with clean clothes. Either that or from some creep who longs for a meaningful relationship with a healthy athlete with clean clothes.

Use a Broker

The words "broker" and "parasite" are usually interchangeable. The broker brings no special skill to a customer nor does he create any product you can see, touch, feel, put into your pocket, or taste. But if you don't have time to scour the classifieds, peruse bulletin boards, or talk to merchants in your neighborhood of choice, use a real estate broker. Just be aware of the pros and cons before you get involved. Aside from the obvious benefits, there can be some problems. If a broker wants you to sign a written contract, make sure it is not an exclusive agreement that requires you to pay his fee even if you rent an apartment through another broker or from your own sources. If the broker insists upon an exclusive agreement make sure it is for no longer than thirty or sixty days, at the longest. Most brokers will actively make an effort to find an apartment for a customer within the first two weeks of the customer signing on board. After that, it is just "another listing" for the broker.

The best thing about brokers is that they do all the work (some people think this is the only good thing about brokers). A good broker will ask detailed questions about what you want and can afford, preview apartments, then show you realistic options. This saves you time and shoe leather. In addition, you get to see apartments that are not advertised or available elsewhere. These are "exclusive" listings, and every real estate agency has them. This selectivity is one of the chief advantages of using a broker and helps justify your paying for the privilege. And it is a costly luxury or a cheap bargain.

Typically, the broker's fee is paid by the tenant, and can run anywhere from one month's rent to 15 percent of the first year's rent. Like everything else in New York, the amount is negotiable, but usually not by much. Having signed an agreement with the broker, do not try to bypass him by making a private arrangement with the landlord after seeing the apartment. You have about as much chance of beating the broker out of his fee as you would have at having a torrid one-night stand with a girl you picked up at an ecumenical conference. The broker has been screwed over by experts and knows every maneuver possible to do him out of a fee. The result will be that the real estate agency will sue you (something they have done a hundred times before), you will waste time and perhaps money in court, and, in the end, you will still have to pay the fee. However, don't pay the broker's fee too soon. Remember, you do not officially have the apartment until the owner or management company approves the lease. Once you are notified that your application has been accepted, wait until the lease is in your hand before paying the broker.

Bear in mind the free lunch has gone the way of the nickel cigar. Even if the broker tells you that his services will cost you nothing since the landlord will pay the fee, the landlord is not giving freebies. You can be certain that some way, somehow the landlord is factoring this extra cost into your rent. Conversely, if you deal directly with the landlord, his saving a broker's fee can be passed directly on to you.

WHERE DO YOU WANT TO LIVE?

The three most important factors in choosing an apartment in New York are location, location, and location. As soon as you tell somebody your address, they immediately start figuring out how much you make a year and if they want to be your new best friend. If you can't afford to live in a decent neighborhood, there are three solutions to the problem. The first is to have your friends drop you off at the fanciest building in the fanciest neighborhood. When you get out of the car walk up to the doorman and engage him in some esoteric conversation, such as, "Any good hookers living in the building?" While he is discussing the occupations of the various female tenants with you, keep an eye on your friend's car. Once it leaves, you can end the conversation with the doorman and take a subway home.

Another solution is to say you are in the Witness Protection Program and are forbidden to reveal where you live. But you can tell that you saw Henry Kissinger open the door of the next apartment to take in the morning paper as he was talking to Sylvester Stallone who was just coming home to *his* apartment across the hall after a long night of speech lessons. Or you can do what most New Yorkers do: get a lousy apartment in the best neighborhood possible.

The criteria most people use in looking for an apartment are safety, personality, convenience, and affordability.

Safety

Safety is most people's primary concern in looking for an apartment. The nicest apartment in the world loses its charm if you have to share it with a burglar or have to fight your way through a gang war every evening when you come home.

Visit the community liaison officer at the local precinct and ask about crime rates and general safety in the area. He may even be able to tell you the crime statistics of the very building into which you are considering moving. If it is the site of monthly muggers' conventions, you might want to consider taking a pass. Walk around the neighborhood with a friend during the day and at night. If you don't feel comfortable, don't live there.

Personality

Every neighborhood has a personality. Is your preference a formal neighborhood? Laid-back? Young? Geriatric? Professional? Mainly singles or families? What about ethnicity? Chinese, Italian, Indian, Russian, Jewish, Greek, Irish, Jamaican—New York has more nationalities than Macy's has panty hose.

In some neighborhoods, people keep up with local events by hanging out on their stoops and schmoozing with their neighbors. Everybody greets one another when they pass on the street. Elsewhere, the doormen don't even talk to one another, and people avoid eye contact when they cross paths. In a New York apartment house elevator most people stare straight ahead and look at Texas. They would rather be shot in the heart than have to actually look at the person next to them. Take the time to find out what feels right to you.

Convenience

Consider what you want nearby. Do you need a supermarket, green market, massage parlor, or pharmacy? What about a park, subway station, gym, or heliport? Do you want to be near the water, a library, or a friendly bar? There are people whose life centers on food and who won't live anywhere but the Upper West Side, so they can be near Zabar's, or near lower Broadway a stone's throw from their morning coffee at Dean & DeLuca. These people would save money by walking around with a feed bag like the horses in Central Park do. This is also a good way to cut down on smoking.

If you want to use the public schools, look into the quality of those closest to your neighborhood of choice. Many districts publish their standardized test results. Ask to see them. Also find out if your kid can keep his bicycle for more than a week before it is stolen.

Affordability

If you are single or married but chased out by your wife or driven out by your brother-in-law, the secret to affording the apartment you want is simply to turn your perfectly situated one-bedroom into a two-bedroom and find a roommate to share the rent! It's easy. For a reasonable fee, you can get a temporary pressurized wall installed in an apartment. Presto! A new bedroom. The wall leaves when you or the roommate does.

Of course, there are those who believe the walls may be illegal and that you run the risk of contracting tuberculosis from breathing the air in the small, dark, windowless room you have created. Nevertheless, the Living Space in Newark, New Jersey, is doing a land-office business installing temporary walls (201-824-0636).

How to Avoid Getting Mugged in New York

If you walk down certain New York City streets at night, where you should not be in the first place, getting mugged is as certain as missing a subway when you are in a hurry to get to work. Some of these neighborhoods are so dangerous that policemen walk in pairs and carry around change to give to muggers if they are held up. Nothing is guaranteed as a preventative, short of tooling around in a Sherman tank. But the following are some proven suggestions that might come in handy.

Walk around with a paper cup as if you are a homeless person. When you think a guy looks like a mugger, walk over to him with your paper cup and say, "How about it, can you spare anything?" If he doesn't give you any money, it also helps to look menacingly at him as if you are about to mug *him*. The paper cup method works every time unless, of course, you happen to bump into a guy who happens to be in the paper cup business and he is trying to mug people for paper cups. Then, you might have a big problem.

It pays to take a cup with you everywhere you go because you never know. The cup can serve two purposes. One, it could prevent you from getting mugged and two, if business is a little slow, people might throw some money into your cup to help you out. So you might be making a living at the same time you are avoiding a mugging.

Another way to avoid a mugging is to approach the prospective mugger and tell him you are involved in a desperate situation. You are trying to buy more bullets for your gun. Tell him you are down to the last seven bullets and you want to kill at least five other people before the day is over. If he asks you why, if you want to kill only five people, do you need seven bullets? Tell him the reason is you usually miss two out of seven shots. But now you want to use the two extra bullets for practice shots, and look at him like he might be one of the two practice targets.

Since nobody will want to steal an empty wallet, another way to avoid a mugging is to pretend that you were just mugged. Look like a homeless person; take a bottle of ketchup, and throw it in your face to look like you are still bleeding. Tell your prospective mugger that you have just been mugged and you have to get back home to Cuba as fast as possible and need $2,500 because that's how much it takes to get there. Wipe the ketchup off your face while you are talking to him and start putting it on his mouth, and rubbing it all over him. He will say to himself, "A homeless guy with diseases is putting his blood on me. I'm probably going to die from this." He will take out all his money and give it to you as fast as possible to get rid of you or he will run like a thief and thank God he got away from you in time.

Don't wear socks. This will be absolute proof to a prospective mugger that you have no money. Anybody with any sort of money, at least, has a pair of socks—unless they come from California.★

Dress in a disheveled fashion and walk over to a guy who looks like he might be a mugger and say to him, "Hey, do I look like a mugger to you—or like a cop trying to look like a mugger?" Unfortunately the other guy might be a cop himself, also in a mugger's uniform. If that is the case, in ten seconds he will have you arrested for impersonating a cop. If this happens, you were better off being mugged.

★There, if you wear socks, you are unfashionable. However, you don't save any money by not wearing socks since, by not wearing socks, your shoes will wear out sooner.

How to Get a Seat on the Subway When It's Packed and You Can't Get a Seat

Getting a seat on the subway when it's packed is one of the great tricks of all time, because people would rather give up their girlfriend, their sister, their mother, their family, their white shirts in the closet, their last chance to get into a toilet than their seat. You never see fights like when they rush for that slot on the bench. You would think someone was giving away hundred dollar bills.

These people didn't come from a hike, they came from an office where they were sitting for eight hours, so you would think they would want to stand for a few minutes. But they would rather stand anyplace in the world as long as it's not on the subway. On the subway, somehow, the rush to sit down will make them crush anyone who is in their way. You heard about the gold rush. The gold rush was nothing compared to

the rush to get a seat on the subway. And as soon as people get those seats, they guard them with their lives.

They sit there like their asses were attached to the seat and somebody would think that if they got up, they would automatically catch a rare disease and that their next stop would be a cemetery. Or that somehow, somebody is going to bury them because there would be nothing to live for if they lost a seat on the subway.

The trick, therefore, is to be able to get a seat away from somebody already occupying one. This is not easy. Everybody standing is looking down with resentment on the people who are sitting. The people sitting are looking at the floor trying to pretend they don't notice the people standing, because no matter what condition they are in, they don't want to face the possibility that somebody else really *needs* a seat. Even if their own fathers are standing there, swaying in their walkers, they wouldn't give up their seats. They would say, "Wait a second, he didn't do *that* much for me that he deserves a seat. Maybe he raised me, maybe he supported me, maybe he starved to be able to pay so that I could afford a token and get in the subway and have a job, and if it was not for him, I wouldn't be living. But just because I owe him my life doesn't mean I owe him my seat on the subway. There is a limit to how much you owe a person just for making it possible for me to live on this earth. If he wants my money, he can have it, but not my seat." So people stand there and stand and stand some more and all the time think of ways to get that seat.

One of the best ways is to pretend that you are drunk. There is no way anybody can prove you are not drunk, and to make sure you prove your point, start fumbling and shuffling around on your feet like you're about to fall down any second. To make it more realistic, actually fall down right next to the person seated, and if that doesn't work, go further—fall down right on top of him. You can't hit a drunken person, since hitting a helpless drunken person is like hitting a two-year-old child, and everybody in the subway would grab the guy by the throat and wipe him out in a second (although their extension might not extend so far as to then let you have the seat *they* fought for). On the other hand, you don't want to lie there on top of the guy unless it is just your good luck that you fell on a homosexual person and he might enjoy it so much that he doesn't want to let you get off. Then again you might be enjoying it too if you have the same inclinations.

If you fall on a girl, you might get lucky. It might be a beautiful girl. She might not enjoy the idea of your lying across her lap, but what do you care, you're having a good time. She might try to push you off, but you can continue to pretend you're drunk. A drunken person can't get up. It's not your fault that you can't stand, and by the time she finally rolls you off her, you will have gotten as lucky as someone who would resort to this tactic could ever hope to get. And you sat down for a moment. A seat is important, but, after all, a sex life, no matter how pathetic, is even more important.

If the "drunken" idea doesn't work, try eating garlic. Every time you go on the subway put a piece of garlic in your mouth. The best way to get rid of any person occupying a seat is to ask him questions with the letter *H* in them, because *H* requires a lot of breath. As you are spewing your breath into the guy's nose, chances are you are slowly asphyxiating him. You can ask questions like, "How do I get to Humboldt Street?" If that doesn't work, substitute "Houston Street" or "Irving Place." From there you can go to the numbers: "One Hundred and Fifth Street and One Hundred and Sixth Street." The great thing about this question is that the city has several hundred numbered streets, so you can go on like this for a while if need be. This strategy will always work unless, just your luck, the man may work in an Italian restaurant and like the smell of used garlic.

Another idea is to try coughing, especially if you are wearing a dirty shirt. Take a dirty shirt with you and preferably make sure that the shirt is not only dirty but your hands are dirty, too, and then if you start coughing the guy will figure you must have a rare disease. A person seated might be willing to tolerate a guy who is loud and annoying. However, if he thinks he is catching something, and if a guy like the one standing over him starts coughing when everybody reads in the paper about the spread of tuberculosis and Ebola, then the person must be thinking, "This is it, I don't want to give up my seat, but if my life is involved. . . ." Then he starts thinking about his family—his wife and children. Okay, maybe not his wife, but at least his children. And he will say to himself, "I'd better get the hell out of here."

If the coughing doesn't work because the person seated is too stupid to think of becoming diseased, try sneezing, and if the sneezing doesn't work, start spitting. Sooner or later the combination of these three will finally impel the person seated to get up and say, "It's up to you pal." That's New Yorkese for "God bless you."

Another good idea is to pretend that you have fleas. Something is itching from somewhere and you can't quite find the spot, as if a cockroach is crawling around your body and you have to find it and you're pulling ticks and things off you, but the cockroach is always one step ahead, and the seated person doesn't know if you have anything in your hands or not and wonders where they are landing and whether he is going to catch the same condition. Nobody wants to keep guessing, so he decides it is easier to get off the subway than to keep wondering what kind of disease is being thrown at him. The great thing about all this is that there is no way a person can call a cop and there is no way to call for help. The only way he can do anything about this is to get off the seat.

Of course, once you have the seat you must keep swaying drunkenly, sneezing, spitting, scratching, whatever. You wouldn't want anyone to try those same tricks to get your seat.

How to Save Money
on Vegetables

Jewish people have developed a method for saving money when ordering vegetables in a restaurant. It is best illustrated by showing how differently Jews and gentiles deal with the problem.

When gentiles go into a restaurant and order food they are always wasting money because when they order vegetables they simply say, "Give me vegetables." You have to be stupid to simply say, "Give me vegetables." Vegetables cost a fortune today, and there is no reason to pay that much money when there is a way you can get them for nothing.

Notice that Jews never say just, "Give me vegetables." They always ask one important question which saves a fortune. "Do the vegetables come with the dinner or not?" If they are not on the dinner, it's, "Yek, I hate vegetables, there is nothing more I hate more than vegetables," but you can get nauseous when you hear, "Oh, they're on the dinner? Put it down, put

it down, put it down. What kind of vegetables you got today? Cauliflower, yek, I hate cauliflower. Oh, they're on the dinner, oh, put it down. Put it down no matter what kind of vegetables, put it down, put it down." Then somebody in your party will always say, "Yek, I hate cauliflower." "Keep your mouth shut. The waiter does not need to know that you hate cauliflower. You can have whatever you want, don't worry about it. I'll take the corn, I'll give you the cabbage; you give me the cauliflower, I'll give you the salad; you give me the carrots, I'll give you my peas." Before you know it, vegetables are coming and going all around the table.

Another way to save money in New York is, after dining and the meal is over, start packing. When gentiles believe the meal is over they just go home. Jews don't just go home, they start packing. Every Jew says the same thing at the end of a dinner. "Do me a favor, sweetheart, if you don't mind, put this in a bag." And before you know it they start packing and the packing takes longer than the meal. Everything they see goes into a bag. "If you don't mind put it into a bag. What's on the other table? They're finished already, they don't need it. Put it in a bag. Got anything left over in the kitchen, put it in a bag. How about this chair? Put it in the bag."

Whatever they see, they put it in a bag. Jews come into a restaurant weighing seven pounds they come out weighing nine hundred pounds with bags and bags. They don't look like they went eating. They look like they went shopping.

Korean Delis

Over the past twenty-five years the mom-and-pop delis have become mama-san-and-papa-san twenty-four-hour-a-day family-style stores that masquerade under the name of delis. Replacing the moms and pops that came here from Poland or Sicily are Korean families, who are, to an ordinary New Yorker's eyes, unsophisticated and, to be perfectly frank and perhaps not unclouded by prejudice, indistinguishable from one another. These delis, selling everything from condoms to cantaloupes at noncompetitive prices, have about as much in common with old-fashioned delis as your kitchen knife does with an overpriced Swiss army knife with four thousand gadgets.

If it appears to you that you see the same products and produce at the same price in all the Korean delis, you are correct. Previously, in New York, if a second deli opened within five blocks of another, a deli war was declared. Pickles and pastrami flew, and the streets ran red with ketchup. The war continued until one store or the other turned yellow, or at least mustard color, and threw in the floor mop.

The Koreans came up with a better idea. The stores are mostly owned by groups of families. Often three or four families will own all of the stores in a ten-block area. Families do not share the profits with one another, but they do cooperate with each other economically by forming "*gays*." A *gay* has nothing to do with queer money or anything of a lavender nature. Rather, it is a system whereby each family contributes as much as a thousand dollars a week into a fund. When there is a desire to open a new deli, a member of the *gay* can make an interest-free loan with the other members of the *gay* as partners.

All of the stores buy the same goods at the same price from one or two large wholesale commissaries. The same merchandise, with the same brand names, is then sold at the same price in all of the Korean delis. This system was devised by Won Limp Wang, who has, because of his efforts, become a national hero in Korea. Each year they celebrate Wang's birthday on Yom Kippur as a national holiday. The truth is that Wang's birthday does not really fall on Yom Kippur, but the ever clever Korean businessmen realized that since Jews are not out shopping in Korean markets on Yom Kippur, it would be a good day to have a holiday and take it easy.

COMMON SCAMS

The Zeroing the Scale Scam

Every salad bar in a Korean deli has a scale used to weigh the various prepared salad ingredients selected by the consumer. The good news is, the scales are regulated by the Department of Consumer Affairs. It might surprise some to learn that the Consumer Affairs Department is not a city agency comprised of men who are sleeping with customers. Rather it is a city watchdog agency. The bad news is, the commission has ten agents to check all the metered scales in New York City. This is a little like expecting a midget to give all the girls in a harem a good time. Although each scale has an embossed metal seal of approval from the city, the inspection may have taken place sometime between when Peter Stuyvesant was governor and the Civil War riots.

To avoid paying for the deli owner's thumb each time one buys salad, care must be taken to make sure the scale reads zero before anything is placed on it. After the empty container is put on the scale, it must be recalibrated to a new zero point.

The Large Chunk Scam

One of Confucius's proverbs is, "He who cut food into big chunk, make most money at salad bar."

Unless you are in desperate need of a forty-pound black olive with a thirty-six-pound pit, cucumber slices the size of sewer covers, and carrots that would give Bugs Bunny a hernia, make sure the salad ingredients are cut into as many small pieces as possible.

The deli owners love to sell the salad in large pieces because: (a) the customer will have to get a bigger container to fit them all in—once they are in a bigger container, they will all look smaller and the impulse will be to fill the vacant spaces with more salad; and (b) bigger pieces may result in buying more than you ordinarily would need. If there were lots of little pieces a customer could stop when he feels he has just enough.

The Fresh Fruit Scam

If fresh fruit is going to be used in the salad, one should be aware that the fresh fruit sold in the premade, prepacked containers is usually less expensive than the fresh fruit reposing in the salad bar. The only problem with prepackaged fruit salad is, very often the salad has been turned into an apartment house for bugs.

Therefore, look through the transparent container very carefully before purchase. If anything is moving in the container, either take it for a walk or pick another container.

Often the salad dressings are a mixture of whatever chemicals are left over from the salad dressings featured the previous day. The sign NO MSG OR PRESERVATIVES is as truthful as is a new girlfriend who says, "I have never done anything like this before."

The best advice on salad dressing is to keep a bottle of purchased dressing in the refrigerator at home or at work. Then, at least, the consumer can learn from the label which chemicals he or she is ingesting. To paraphrase Hamlet, "Better to accept the chemicals you know, than fly to others that you know not of."

Freshness Scam

If one cares about freshness, the best advice, aside from, "Start dating teenagers with pimples," is to try to choose daily from the same salad bar at the same deli. By comparing with other items in the salad compartment, one gets to recognize—if not develop a speaking acquaintance with—the old salad. The rule of thumb is that the fresh salad is usually at the bottom of the bin, and the old salad is put on the top. Furthermore, the refrigeration is coldest at the bottom, so one doubly stands a better chance of avoiding a stomach pump by digging down.

HOT FOOD

Try to choose hot food from a steam table that has a thermometer visible to the consumer. New York State law directs that food must be kept at a temperature of at least 140° Fahrenheit. At lower temperatures, all the owner has done is to create a cozy environment for bacteria. And while one might believe, except for unemployed brothers-in-law, everybody should live and be well, it is not imprudent to make a similar exception for bacteria.

SELECTION

The Korean delis have most of the products you can find at your local supermarket. They often also have a rather consistent variety of European epicurean treats. The downside is that one pays for the privilege of shopping at odd hours at a convenient location. The following are comparisons of deli prices for some common items with the prices charged at a representative supermarket.

Item	Korean Deli	Sloan's
Milk, 1 qt.	$ 2.00	$ 1.40
Cereal (Special K, 14 oz.)	6.00	4.00
Budweiser six-pack	9.00	6.50
Häagen-Dazs, 1 pt.	4.00	3.25
1 bottle soda, 1 lt.	2.25	.99
Kitty Litter 10 lb. bag	3.99	2.49
tuna fish (small tin)	4.00	1.69
toilet paper (Charmin, four-pack)	2.99	1.09

The best approach is—unless you need to satisfy a craving for a dozen red roses at one dollar each at two o'clock in the morning—to purchase at a deli only those items that, of necessity, can only be purchased at a particular time and comparison shop for the rest.

Middle Eastern
Electronic Stores

Periodically, various city agencies crack down on the combination electronic, camera, and computer stores that dot the Big Apple, particularly those in the parts of the city tourists visit. A visitor has no trouble spotting these stores, usually owned by Syrians, since they all have large going-out-of-business signs in their windows. If they do not have going-out-of-business signs, they have signs that say in large letters CLOSING STORE. Then, at the bottom of the sign, in letters the size of the last line on an eye chart, the printing reads, 11:00 P.M. TONIGHT.

These stores are so crooked that only hunchbacks can walk in standing up. Sometimes the Syrians who own the stores put shredded newspapers on the floor to enhance the feeling that they are going out of business. This presents an additional advantage to the consumer. You can bring your puppy in to be housebroken while you are being robbed.

CRACKING THE PRICE CODE

These stores have thirty different prices for each item. The salesmen size you up when you walk in, and the price of the item
you want varies with his assessment of you. If you are wearing
nice shoes, it is $30; a cheap tie . . . $10; an expensive watch . . .
$70; if you had a good nose job . . . $120; a bad nose job . . .
$26. If you look like you just came from the airport wearing a
polyester shirt . . . $9,000. The pricing code varies from store
to store, but here are the most common and still frequently
used codes.

SCAMS

Stock Number Scam

On the back of the display model of the item you want to buy
(let's say a Sony Walkman), look for the price tag. The ticket
will have an extremely inflated price, like $189.99. Right under-
neath that price should be another number that looks like a
stock number. This number starts with a 9 and ends with a 9
(e.g., 91009). Ignore the nines and divide the remaining number
by two! If the tag on the Walkman had the number 91009,
then you know that the lowest price the store would sell it to
you for is $50.00!

Letter Code Scam

Instead of the bogus "stock number," the price tag might carry
some letters. Let us assume we are dealing with the same Walkman with the same inflated price of $189.99, and underneath
that number are printed the letters *FA*. To crack their code,
follow this chart:

A B C D E F G H I J
0 1 2 3 4 5 6 7 8 9

Each letter corresponds with a number. For example, the letters *FA* tell the salesman that the lowest price for the Walkman is $50.

Gray Market Scam

When we say "gray market," we are not talking about an outdoor vegetable market on a cloudy day. We are talking about buying an item that was manufactured for distribution in southern Zambia. The item may well be identical to the item sold in New York, but the warranty that comes with it is only good in Rhodesia.

Compounding the problem is that many of these stores will not refund or even exchange merchandise, even if you bought it thirty seconds earlier. The way to avoid gray market goods is to examine the warranty. If the description of the item in the box is in Swahili, then your best bet is to let a loyal Kikuyu tribesman buy it while you walk over to a more reputable place.

The Lunch Box Scam

Most of these unscrupulous stores use another technique called "lunching" a box. The scam is that the item you are buying as new has already been used by someone else and returned for some reason or other. It might also mean that the store has opened the box, removed some of the contents, and closed the box again. They might take out the AC adapter, the carrying case, or battery. They will then try to sell the missing items to you as extras. To avoid a "lunched" box, inspect the box to make sure that it is still sealed with the factory package seals!

The Refurbished Scam

Many times these stores will buy factory refurbished goods. If you bought a Sony Walkman, and it did not work properly, you might send it back to Sony. Sony would send you a new one, but they would then repair the one you sent back and offer it to a retailer as factory reconditioned. When the retailer gets it, it comes with a red sticker on the box that states it has been reconditioned. The store then uses an ordinary hair dryer (that they will also subsequently sell as new to some other sucker) to heat up the adhesive. Presto, the sticker comes off without a mark while the Syrian blow-dries his hair at the same time. The store then gets to charge you the normal price for something that it purchased for one half the wholesale price. You end up with a used, broken, then repaired Walkman with no factory warranty!

A lot of the larger chain stores cannot practice this type of deception; however, if they say that they will beat any competitor's price, check first. Who they consider a competitor may be a second-hand store located in the outskirts of Pittsburgh.

If you have a question about a place you are about to do business with, contact the Better Business Bureau (212-533-6200). However, if you are purchasing the item at night or on weekends—the best time of day for both cockroaches and Syrians—nobody will be home at the bureau. Your next best bet is to stick with large chain stores. Use a credit card, since the credit card companies will either refund the money or get on the back of the retailer to adjust the problem. Examine the packaging of the items you buy and if any appear to be tampered with, take a pass, no matter how much of a steal you think you're getting. Ask about the store's return policy and, of course, always save all the wrappings, receipts, instructions, etc.

Parking Signs

It is easier for a man to admit to his wife he is wrong about the price he paid for a mink coat or even a building than to admit he made a mistake in anything that has to do with a car. No husband will confess he is wrong when he is looking for directions, parking a car, or regarding anything else having to do with his driving. When he's behind the wheel, no husband would ever admit he has no idea where he is going or what he is talking about. That's why when a husband and wife look at a parking sign in mid-Manhattan—signs so confusing even Einstein would have trouble deciphering them—the couple is more likely to get a divorce now than if the wife were to walk in on him while he was exchanging vital body fluids with his manicurist. As soon as a happily married couple look at one of those parking signs a divorce lawyer can start making plans to buy *his* happily married wife a new diamond ring. If divorce lawyers in Manhattan could finagle it, they would have their offices within yards of parking signs for the convenience of their future clients.

This would also be a great place to have a psychiatrist's office

because, all of a sudden, every complex the couple ever had breaks out when they start fighting about the parking sign.

It would be also a great place for a drugstore. You probably could sell huge amounts of aspirin to all the people who wind up with vicious headaches while trying to figure out parking signs.

The signs never say the same thing from one line to the other. The signs read as if they were written by anti-Semites just to confuse Jewish people. Here is an actual sign on Fifth Avenue and Fifty-seventh Street:

NO PARKING ANYTIME

NO STANDING

7 A.M.–6 P.M.

MON.–FRI.

HOUR PARKING 6 P.M.–12 A.M.

---

8 A.M.–12 A.M.

SAT. AND SUN.

25¢ PER 15 MIN.

QUARTERS AND NYCTA TOKENS

TOW AWAY ZONE

A husband and wife get out of the car and look at the sign— for the next hour and a half. It is for them one of the greatest riddles of all time. As a matter of fact, if people had any intelligence they would take the bus instead. People say they don't want to take a bus because it makes too many stops. But all the stops put together don't take one tenth as long as the stop you make in front of the parking sign to figure out if it's legal to park there or not. You could walk from your house to wherever you are going a lot faster than you could figure out what it says on the sign.

The sign always starts off with NO PARKING ANYTIME, so you figure you might as well go home. But if you read the second line on the sign, already you are stuck for another month because the second line says NO STANDING. So you say, "What has standing got to do with it? We are talking about *parking* a car. Is the sign aimed at people *standing* or is it aimed at people *parking*?" Then further down, the sign simply says 7 A.M.–6 P.M. MON.–FRI. What does that mean? Are they the work hours according to the hooker's union rules? If the sign says NO PARKING ANYTIME, then why does it have to say NO PARKING WEDNESDAYS? To make matters worse it then says HOUR PARKING 6 P.M.–12 A.M. and ends with TOW AWAY ZONE. You keep wondering, Where is the tow away zone? You know you are allowed to park on Tuesdays and Thursdays, and maybe Wednesdays and Fridays, so when do they tow the car away? Do they tow the car away only on the other days? But which days can these be if the top line on the sign says NO PARKING ANYTIME? But then it also says, SAT. AND SUN. 8 A.M.–12 A.M. On another sign twenty paces away, the sign says ALTERNATE PARKING TUESDAYS, FRIDAYS AND WEDNESDAYS. If you're trying to figure it out, you can't park at all Mondays, Wednesdays, and Fridays, alternate parking Thursdays, Tuesdays, and Sundays; and you don't know if there is alternate parking or if that refers to the same days, the other days or all those days. Then there's our favorite sign reading NO PARKING BETWEEN SIGNS. Which signs do they mean? Between this sign and the one on a corner in Canarsie?

Now a fight immediately breaks out between the husband and wife and they are still attacking each other when finally they see a guy walking toward them. They say, "Mister, can you figure out this sign? It says Tuesdays, Thursdays, Fridays, Sundays? Which is it?"

The guy says, "You can't park."

The wife then attacks the guy. "What do you mean you can't park?"

He says, "Can't you see it says no parking anytime?"

Then she starts a fight with him. "But it says you're allowed to park Mondays."

He says, "This is Tuesday."

The husband says, "So what if it's Tuesday? It says, tow away zone. Tow away zone means you can't park at any time; but, this is not the tow away zone, the tow away zone is some-place else."

"Where is it?"

"I don't know. It doesn't say on the sign."

"What does it say?"

The guy pleads, "What do you want from me, I am not from this neighborhood."

"Then why are you offering me advice in the first place?"

Then this poor guy is saying, "How did I get involved?"

And then the *husband* attacks the guy. " 'How did *I* get involved?' *I* did not get involved, we just asked you a question."

"Tell your wife she doesn't know what she's talking about."

"Who do you think you are to talk that way to my wife?"

And then the guy says, "I'll talk that way to whoever I please."

Now not only is the couple in a fight, but there is also a stranger in a fight with both of them, and each is threatening to kill the other. So criminal lawyers could also make a living here by the parking signs.

Finally, the trio calls a truce by saying, "Let's go into a store. The storekeeper must know, that's his field. He has the store here. He should know if you are allowed to park or not."

They go into the store. "What do you think, mister, are you allowed to park here or not?"

The storekeeper says, "You *could* park here."

"When?"

"I don't know exactly when but I know you could park here."

"But will you get a ticket?"

He says, "Oh, a ticket, this I don't know. I see there is room for parking, but I don't know when they give a ticket."

The husband says, "Well, how come you don't know? You live here, your store is right here?"

"My store is here, but I'm not a cop, I'm not in charge of parking, I sell shirts. What are you bothering me for? You want to buy a shirt, I'll sell you one, but I don't give out information without a sale of a shirt."

The stranger says, "I give up. Park whenever you want, I got my own troubles."

Passes

After having attended the Democratic and Republican conventions, we appreciated the fact that anytime there are more than fifty gentiles in one place, everybody has to have passes. Gentiles love to hang passes around their necks. A Jewish man spends two thousand dollars for a suit with a matching shirt and socks, just so he can feel important. A gentile doesn't have to have his jacket match his pants or even have one leg of his trousers match the other. He knows that this is his country, so his looking like he got dressed in a closet without a light doesn't bother him. When he is in a large crowd, if he wants to get into an event, he gets himself a pass to hang around his neck on a chain.

When a Jew wants to get in somewhere, he just pushes to the head of the line, or as he is shoving people out of the way, he is shouting, "Get out of my way. I'm Schwartz New York." Gentiles show their passes. White passes to get into one area, blue for upstairs, yellow for the bathrooms, pink for the lavender seats, brown to be exchanged for violet when the red expires.

While gentiles are matching their colors to where they want to go and are exchanging and trading different-colored passes with one another, the Jews are going over to the ushers and giving them ten dollars to sit anywhere.

Whenever a popular rock group comes to New York, to obtain any ticket not in the "Ray Charles" section (the part of the balcony where you can hear everything but can't see anything) requires either being born into the family of one of the performers or being prepared to exchange relatives for tickets. The better looking the relative is, the better the ticket you get. If you offer your brother-in-law, they will throw him back.

We have developed a mechanism that not only will get you a place close enough to be hit with the sweat coming off the performers or stoned from the slightly used pot, but you will also actually be able to go backstage and hang out with the band.

Let us assume that the latest hot rock group Vomit and the Four Viruses is performing at Madison Square Garden. Seats can be obtained through Ticketmaster, but basically these are tickets for seats where you would be sitting on the outskirts of Cincinnati. But, at least, the Ticketmaster ticket will get you through the door at Madison Square Garden.

Our scheme is based on the fact that any large venue, like Madison Square Garden, hires its own security. These security people, who are most likely union workers and who have been doing this sort of thing for years, are not hired by the rock group.

Most backstage passes for rock concerts are in some way a variation of the event's poster or the cover of the group's latest album. Utilizing this knowledge, together with Kinko's as a co-conspirator, you will have no problem in getting backstage. Just follow these easy steps.

1. Bring the cover of the *current* CD (front and back) of the artist or group to Kinko's. They will reduce it 25 percent for about $2.00.

2. Go to the computer section of Kinko's. Using their computer, print up a page that says ALL ACCESS using a font that works best (we like the one called Stencil). Have Kinko's transfer that printout onto red paper (at a price of $1.50, including computer time and printing).

3. Cut out the color copy of the album cover you made (see step 1) and cut out the ALL ACCESS line so that it all fits together. The words ALL ACCESS should be at the bottom of the album cover.

4. Glue the whole thing together very artistically.

5. Have Kinko's laminate it for you while you wait ($2.50).

6. Use a hole puncher to punch a hole in the top for a chain.

7. Hang the pass from your neck with a chain (purchased from the five-and-ten, $.50).

Total Price: $6.50
Total Time: 20 minutes

When you get to the concert, you produce only your purchased ticket for admission, keeping the newly created pass concealed inside your shirt until needed. When you go backstage, sporting the pass around your neck, be forewarned that the backstage crew and security there were hired by the artists (and usually will not be fooled by your pass), so flash it quickly with a casual self-assurance and don't linger around them!

Enjoy the show, and since you are now an insider, you may end up with one of the groupies rocking you to sleep. And the sleep you sleep will be that of the righteous. You have not cheated anybody nor done anything illegal, immoral, or fattening. You have paid for your ticket and merely been able to circulate with your fellow artists backstage. The worst that can happen, in the usual course, is for you to be thrown out of the arena. If the management decides not to act "in the usual course," don't call us. We'll call you.

Restaurant Reservations

It is as difficult to get a dinner reservation in a good restaurant in New York—particularly one that has been mentioned in newspaper columns, received a rave review from critics, or has been the scene of a gangland slaying—as it is to find an honest politician in Washington or at least a Presbyterian minister at a bar mitzvah. We are going to reveal the secret of getting a table in a hot restaurant. This information alone is worth the price of this book.

The key to getting a table is the knowledge that, even though a restaurant is fully booked, for people important to the management, room will be found. Ordinarily, if you want to go to Sardi's after the theater, or decide at ten minutes to seven to have a seven o'clock dinner at Le Cirque, or dine at any number of French restaurants with maître d's who look at you as if they just opened a refrigerator and smelled last Tuesday's milk, you would have as much chance of getting into these restaurants as you would have of getting into Sharon Stone. But come closer, listen carefully, and follow these simple rules, and

you will not only be in the restaurant quicker than Willie Sutton got into a bank vault but also you will get the best table in the house.

Call the restaurant and say you are calling for one of the following columnists: Richard Johnson, Neil Travis, Cindy Adams, George Rush, Liz Smith, etc. Tell the person you speak to that the columnist will be over with a party of six in ten minutes. Even if the restaurant is entirely filled they will make room for you.

When you arrive you will see tourists from Peoria, Illinois, and BQEs (Brooklyn–Queens Expressway) out for a special evening that they booked early in February 1935, still desperately clutching their napkins, being flung out the doors and windows, to make room for your party. Once you get past the flying tourists, ask for Mr. Johnson's, Mr. Travis's, Miss Smith's, Mr. Rush's, or Ms. Adams's table. The waiters will plow through the crowd like General Patton going through Germany, while you explain that the columnist is on the way and will shortly join the party.

Having now been seated at the best table in the house, while the angry tourists outside the restaurant are getting together suicide squads to assassinate you when you leave the restaurant and the other diners in the restaurant are staring at you with a mixture of jealousy and hatred reserved for understudies watching the star perform on opening night, excuse yourself from the table, citing a call from nature. Instead of the bathroom, your destination should be the nearest telephone. Making sure nobody can overhear you, call the restaurant and ask for the maître d'. Explain to him that you are calling for the columnist, who is on deadline and is confounded by a recalcitrant muse and therefore cannot join his or her friends. You can even say, when you call, you are the columnist him- or herself, since hardly anyone knows what they sound like, particularly on the telephone over the din of a noisy restaurant. Needless to say, if your name is Gustave and you have a mustache, it would be foolhardy to say you are Cindy Adams. If you are adventurous you can make up additional reasons why the columnist could not meet his or her friends at the restaurant. "The cement in Ms. Adams's hair is not dry yet," or "Ms. Adams had an accident. She bent over to pick something up, and the weight of her hair propelled her to the floor. She cannot budge and they have had to send out for three gentiles with tools to raise her head off the floor, so she will be delayed." Actually Cindy Adams may be a poor choice. She seldom goes to restaurants because, at her age (over thirty) she is so drop-dead gorgeous that her life is in danger from every Jewish wife in the place.

Once you explain that circumstances prevent you from joining your party, be sure to ask the maître d' to "take good care of my friends." Additionally, although we absolutely do not advise you to do the following, you are probably such a cheap low-life bastard that this is just what you will want to do—namely, indicate that it would be appreciated if the management would pick up the bill and suggest that the restaurant will get an enormous plug in your column. If the restaurant is unreceptive to your suggestion, then you would also undoubtedly be low enough to tell them to simply "Put it on my bill."

If you are seeking a table at a restaurant in an outer borough, or even the suburbs, utilizing the name of a columnist will have less effect. In Queens, you might suggest you are John Gotti's nephew; in Brooklyn, introduce yourself as the illegitimate son of President Reagan. One name that seems to work everywhere is Sylvester Stallone.

One last suggestion; leave a big tip. You don't want to make your host look like a cheapskate.

Sickness as a
Survival Weapon

The secret of karate is to turn your adversary's strength to your advantage. Similarly, to survive in New York, the secret is to make every adversity, every misfortune, every misery work to your benefit.

One of the most powerful of all survival weapons is sickness. Not everyone has the good fortune to be sick at any particular time. But let's be honest. As soon as you hear that someone else is sick, you feel happy it is not you who is sick. The sicker the other person is, the happier you feel. Then you feel guilty about being happy, and after that you imagine yourself being sick—and other people being happy about your misfortune and the problems you can have and the help you might need if you became sick. Out of all this mishmash of emotions comes a bread-upon-the-waters philosophy resulting in a desire to be of assistance to the sick or unfortunate. Let us examine how this dynamic affects some of the usual activities of life in New York.

THE TELEPHONE COMPANY

Your phone goes on the fritz. You go call the repair service (using a neighbor's telephone to make the call, since the odds in favor of finding a pay phone that works are about the same as the Grand Rabbi of Jerusalem cornering the market on pickled pigs' knuckles). You bounce around from person to person, recording to recording. In the process of listening to recorded messages you receive a crash course in the federal antitrust law that was designed to protect the consumer but ended up costing him twice as much in time and telephone calls as he conceivably could have saved by having five companies do the work that one company used to do. You finally get the repair service on the phone. After being asked, "Is it the instrument, the box in your apartment, or the line itself?" you politely explain that if you were a telephone engineer you would not be calling them in the first place. The question of actually arranging a repair appointment comes up. The lobotomized voice on the other end informs you that a repairman will arrive at your home between nine and five next August twenty-seventh.

At this point you carefully explain to the voice that you have a serious cardiac condition, with a heart-lung machine and a donor ready to hand over his heart standing by. Therefore, in an emergency you must be able to call Dr. DeBakey. In a flash the operator will tell you that they will have a repairman at your house within three hours—which probably explains why everybody who did not buy this book will have to wait until August twenty-seventh to have their phone repaired.

The reason the above suggestion works is, in addition to all the psychological and humanitarian reasons involved in going out of one's way to help a less fortunate fellow, there is the very real concern that if the customer really did get a heart attack and was unable to telephone for a doctor and died, the deceased's estate would make another call. This would be on a phone that does work, and it would be to a friendly neighborhood lawyer, who, for a modest percentage, would sue the underwear off the phone company.

The fact that you might need a telephone to *receive* calls because of misfortune or illness is also effective.

"My husband is scheduled to be executed at midnight tonight and we are waiting to receive a call from the governor commuting his sentence."

"I am a surgeon and must be ready to operate at the drop of a hat or fallopian tube if necessary."

You might also need to receive a telephone call because of high national purpose.

"I work for the CIA and must be available to parachute into Cuba instantaneously."

"I am about to be appointed to the Supreme Court and am expecting a call from the president at any moment."

"I am a very high-priced hooker and am expecting a call from the president at any moment."

TELEVISION CABLE REPAIRS

The four corners of your television picture look like they are trying to flee the picture tube in different directions. Obviously, the men working on the cable in the street are using it to take xylophone lessons to learn the pulsating rhythms of salsa. It is claimed that the two biggest secrets of the universe are the formula for Coca-Cola and the recipe for the hydrogen bomb. There is a third: how to get a television cable repairman to come to your home in your lifetime.

The first thing you do is call the cable company a half dozen times complaining about problems with the picture, giving addresses of different buildings in the vicinity of your home but

hanging up before they ask for your name. The purpose of doing this is so that when you make your legitimate call about the problem they cannot say you are the first one to complain. Furthermore, the company has done studies indicating that each call received is representative of a precise number of thousands of subscribers.

When you call, giving your true name and address, you will meet with the inevitable, "A repairman will be at your home before three P.M. next Halloween." At this point you explain that you are an invalid, have been bedridden for the last three years, and are despondent and the only pleasure in your otherwise desolate life is watching television. And, oh yes, your life is so empty and cheerless without your television that you probably will commit suicide . . . but not before you write a note blaming the cable TV company. Usually the repairman will be there before you hang up.

If the invalid ploy doesn't work, explain that you just were released from jail after having served thirty years for stabbing a cable repairman in the heart who came late. You believe they cured you in jail of this unusual affliction, but why test it?

THEATER TICKETS

Acquisition of tickets to a hit Broadway show is a problem unique to New York because, for better or worse—and usually for worse—New York is the theater capital of the world. The wall between a ticket to a hit show and the average New Yorker is so formidable that Mr. Average New Yorker has been to the theater fewer times than a moderately well-heeled chiropodist from the suburbs of Spokane, Washington. Because the stratagems and tactics are so convoluted and the need for backup and contingency plans are so essential in a campaign to obtain theater tickets, resorting to the various sickness scams previously explained is simply not sufficient.

There are conventional ways—all with built-in drawbacks or limitations—to obtain theater tickets, other than buying them at the box office.

Since ticket brokers in New York are limited by law to charging only five dollars or 10 percent over the listed price of a ticket, legitimate brokers in this town are as extinct as bell-bottom trousers. But you can import theater tickets from theater ticket brokers in New Jersey or Connecticut without going through customs. However, you will probably pay more for them than it would cost to smuggle in a pound of opium from Addis Ababa. And at least a box of opium has approximately the same price all over New York. Not a theater ticket. A ticket broker in Fort Lee, New Jersey, selling a ticket to a hit play to a New Yorker gears his price to the particular theatergoer's desire to see a hit show and the thickness of his wallet. From havens in Connecticut and New Jersey (New Jersey legalized scalping in October 1995, under the banner of free trade), the brokers, whose names and telephone numbers are usually contained in small ads in the theater sections of newspapers, sell hit show tickets to New Yorkers at whatever the traffic will bear, usually three or four times the face amount printed on the ticket.

The ticket broker obtains the unobtainable in two different ways, one honest and one dishonest. The overpriced ticket you might be lucky or unlucky enough to have purchased has probably arrived in your eager hand by the dishonest route.

The honest acquisition of tickets by a broker involves the use of "diggers." A digger is usually a poor college student who stands in line at the box office for days at a time with a water bottle and bologna sandwich, through floods and blizzards, doing his homework. He does this for a few dollars in order to buy a handful of tickets (at list price) for the broker. It is suspected that many a great entrepreneurial career got its start when a student bought a couple of pairs of tickets for resale with his own money. Diggers can also do their work by buying advance tickets via mail order. Broadway shows severely limit the sale of tickets to diggers—probably for no better reason than a digger sale removes the management's chance of getting a piece of the illegal action. The show's company managers pride themselves on being able to spot a mail order digger even though the digger might use the name of Count Horglitz von Steiglitz and give a return address in upper Saxony.

The more usual way a broker gets his tickets is by buying a block of choice tickets at the box office. The reason the broker is able to do this is because added on to the price of each ticket he purchases is a "Mafia tax," or, at least, Broadway's version of the Mafia. The broker, purchasing a large number of seats, pays perhaps an extra ten to fifty dollars in cash over and above the legitimate price of the ticket to the box office for each seat. This cash is divided up among all the various managerial people connected with the theater up to, it is rumored, the owners of the theater itself. The performers and artistic people involved in the show see none of these moneys.

Quick arithmetic indicates that when you start adding up the extra bribe money the broker shells out, the cost of hand-delivering the ticket from New Jersey to New York, the cost of advertising, and the broker's profit, you rapidly come to a price for a ticket that would make it cheaper to get on a plane to London where—given the state of the present Broadway theater, the Broadway show probably came from in the first place—and buy a ticket for the same show's original production. London ticket prices are strictly limited by law and are a fraction of the cost of New York tickets.

You can also obtain tickets to a hit show from a hotel concierge. He will pick up a phone and call the same broker in

Fort Lee to get you the tickets. However, now the concierge's profit will be added on to the ticket price, and you probably will pay an additional ten dollars over the broker's already inflated price for that forty-cent telephone call.

Outside every theater or concert hall, twenty minutes before show time, you will probably see characters that would make you want to drink a glass of Pepto-Bismol, selling tickets for that night's performance. These are direct descendants of the people who used to pull you aside to whisper in your innocent ear, "Psst, meester, feelthy pictures," and probably had the tickets printed the night before in a closed-up printing shop in Brooklyn. So unless you want a ticket of admission to a closed-up printing shop in Brooklyn, keep your money in your pocket. Also, both buying and selling these tickets is a crime, and every once in a while the police crack down, creating the possibility, if the state attorney general has his way, that you will spend one of the most unforgettable evenings of your life as a guest of the New York City Department of Correction. Currently what you risk is a fine that adds five hundred dollars to the city coffers and hangs a criminal record on you.

Making Sure You Get the "Best Seats"

Let us assume tickets are available through respectable sources, the question now becomes, Are the seats good ones? Putting aside for the moment Jewish garment manufacturers who would sooner be caught wearing their wives' panty hose than be spotted in a poor seat, what normal person would want to watch a play from a seat in the back of the theater sitting next to a lady with unshaved armpits? Not you, who are a sanitary engineer in matters of personal hygiene. The problem is that the best seats to a hit play have all been sold out from around the time the Monroe Doctrine was signed. There is a way, however, to find happiness, if happiness is every person in the theater eating their hearts out (hence the phrase "a heartless person") when they see where you are sitting.

Look at the ad for the play in the theater section of a newspaper. Since the play's producer is paying for the ad (albeit with other people's money), he will make sure his name appears directly above or below the title of the show—particularly if the show is a hit. If the show is a flop, he would sooner put his name to a newly discovered strain of gonorrhea; but, if it were a flop, you would not need to know his name since you would not be going to see the play in the first place. Because the producer is constantly looking for sucker money for his next show, once you know his name, you will easily find him listed in the telephone directory—and probably also in the Yellow Pages under "Con Men."

Explain to the producer's assistant that you are about to buy a ticket to the show, but the seats available are in the center rear of the orchestra section, and you really need an aisle seat up front. Forget telling her that you need a seat up front because you have a hearing problem, and otherwise you will have to wear your hearing aid. But your hearing aid has an unfortunate tendency to pick up the local Spanish radio station and broadcast the program. It does not bother *you,* but since you are a decent person you are concerned that the people in the adjoining seats may not be fans of Tito Puente and his orchestra. Forget telling her you need an aisle seat because you have a bladder problem requiring you to go to the bathroom every fifteen minutes, or that you are a doctor on call, or that you have hemorrhoids or a bad back and you must get up to stretch every few minutes. They have heard all these pathetic lame excuses before. Saint Vitus' dance is the answer. Unfortunately you suffer from Saint Vitus' dance and are subject to frequent and unexplained fits, accompanied by the involuntary expulsion of an abundance of body fluids. Explain that you would not want to disrupt the show by having to ask a row of people to leave their seats and dry themselves off while you are being carried out.

The thought of an ambulance crew forcibly removing a twitching, jumping, jerking, dripping, frothing-at-the-mouth semilunatic will immediately impel her, right after she attempts to talk you out of going to the show, to give you an aisle seat. Be forewarned; she will tell you how wonderful some of the other shows are, how much better the facilities are in the other theaters for people with your condition, and even offer to treat you to tickets to other shows, etc., all in an attempt to keep you and your condition out of the theater. Stand your ground and indicate this is the only show on Broadway you really want to see (unless you do want free tickets to another show), and you will end up with the treasured up-front aisle seats.

House Seats

Each show reserves a certain number of choice seats for each performance to be sold to celebrities, VIPs, friends and relatives of the cast, etc. These tickets are held until twenty-four hours before a performance, and then, if not ordered, are released for sale to the general public. It is a little-known fact that if the show is not a runaway hit, noncelebrity, insignificant *you* can call the producer's or general manager's office, ask for the person handling house seats, and purchase the best seats in the house for the legitimate price of the ticket. If the show is a hit, you can still call for house seats, but you will have about the same chance of getting them as you will have of booking Dr. Kevorkian to do a one-nighter at Saint Patrick's Cathedral.

"The Booth"

In Duffy Square at Forty-seventh Street and Broadway, in front of the statue of George M. Cohan, complete with a permanently-in-residence New York pigeon relieving itself on the composer's head, there is a simple structure that looks like it was designed by an architect whose specialty is designing the toilets on public beaches. This is TKTS, better known as "the booth," and here tickets go on sale for between 50 and 75 percent off the listed ticket price for literally every Broadway show. The rub is that the tickets only go on sale at 3 P.M. for the same day's performance. For Wednesday and Saturday matinees they go on sale at 10 A.M., and for Sunday matinees at noon. Unless you don't have a life or enjoy standing in the same spot for hours, this is not the place for you. The lines are long and the sun hot or the winds cold, depending on the season. Still, if you are willing to weather these adversities, you can get a great ticket to a flop show or a lousy ticket to a great show at half price. Since tickets are continually being delivered to the booth, if you arrive at 7 P.M., when the line is about gone because everybody has either already purchased their tickets or given up the hope of seeing a show that evening, you may be able to purchase a couple of late-arriving tickets without acquiring sunstroke or at least sore feet.

It should be noted that for those people who can find their way there—and it should not be too difficult if a blind sheikh with a bomb could do it—there is a satellite booth at 2 World Trade Center. Information about tickets on sale at both booths can be obtained by calling 212-768-1818.

Last Minute at the Box Office

It is a little known fact that there is a Broadway rule requiring the box office to hold back four tickets to each performance until thirty minutes before curtain time. These are called emergency tickets. The emergency tickets are intended to prevent two Jews who were victimized by an anti-Semitic computer from coming to blows because they were sold the same seats. By going to the box office half an hour before show time, you

might be able to purchase these tickets or any last-minute returns or tickets that were never picked up.

The Intermission Scam

On the theory that half a show is better than none at all, you can wait for intermission, pick up a *Playbill* lying on the lobby floor, walk in with the crowd, your head heavily immersed in the magazine, and enter the theater. Immediately go to the men's room, unless, of course, that is not your sex of choice. When you hear the show starting, go into the auditorium and give the orchestra section the once-over. Invariably, there will be at least one empty seat. Out of a thousand people, at least *one* will have not liked the show enough to stay for the second act, will have started to have contractions, or at least had a fight with his wife at intermission. Stride confidently to your new seat.

Survival Short Takes

HEART ATTACKS

You do not automatically go to the top of EMS's dance card if somebody calls 911 for an ambulance and tells them you merely have a heart attack. *But,* if you are lucky enough to stop breathing, then the ambulance call will go to the top of the list. Moral: if you want to get quick service it is better to stop breathing than to have a heart attack. Also when you stop breathing, a possible added benefit is that the person who gives you mouth-to-mouth resuscitation might be a twenty-one-year-old blonde.

SAVING ON INSURANCE

New York City has, after Los Angeles, the highest automobile insurance premium rates in the United States. Mayor Giuliani is locked in deadly combat with the insurance companies to force them to lower their rates. He reasons, quite logically, that if the auto theft rate in New York City has been reduced by

50 percent, the insurance premiums New Yorkers pay should be similarly reduced. Otherwise, the companies, by basing their premiums on nonexistent theft statistics, are receiving an unfair windfall at the expense of John Q. Sucker.

Some savvy, semicrooked New Yorkers, who have second or summer homes on Long Island or in New Jersey or Connecticut, believe they have figured out a way to beat the insurance companies. This is a little like trying to beat Nick the Greek at the poker table. But sometimes even Nick loses.

Once you get out of New York City, rates for car insurance premiums drop drastically. If the New York shrewdie has a second home and decides to implement this scam, he registers his car at the address of his second home, claiming that this is where he principally resides and thus is where his car is kept. These people may be concerned that if they have an accident and run over a cat, and the owner sues them for four hundred million dollars claiming that the cat was the reincarnation of Julius Caesar or was, at least, Cleopatra's kitty, and the insurance company will disclaim coverage because of their fraud in obtaining the policy and lying about where they live. Nonetheless they shall feel secure, perhaps through faulty legal advice, that the insurance company's only remedy in situations like these is to collect the difference between the amount of the premium actually paid and what should have been paid. We are not giving legal advice here and recommend you consult an attorney before putting the plot into action yourself. But no matter how the lawyer advises you—and we hope he or she discourages you— putting all questions of legality aside, doing this would make you a member of the Willie Sutton school of morality.

CRASHING AN AFFAIR

From September to July New York City is the capital of the world for charity dinners. Walk into any large hotel on any night of the week and you will find at least half a dozen dinners and receptions listed for the hotel's public rooms. This is not to mention private affairs such as weddings and bar mitzvahs. So numerous are these affairs that, if a particular night is desired, some charities book the date on an annual basis years in advance. It is virtually impossible to book a room at a popular hotel on less than seven months' notice.

In New York, there is an annual dinner for every disease that has ever afflicted mankind and every organization that has more members than can comfortably fit in a telephone booth on a hot day in August. From Mohammedans celebrating the feast of Ramadan to the annual dinner of the Sons of Ireland celebrating the arrival of the spring crop of Four Roses to Jews celebrating the Mad Gefilte Fish Disease, they all have one thing in common. This year's dinner has to outdo last year's. Since there is only a limited amount of time that people will sit still at a dinner and a limited number of courses that can be served, the area where all the effort is expended to outdo last year's dinner is the reception and the smorgasbord served before the main event.

At the smorgasbord there will be a rhinoceros carved out of ice to top last year's elephant sculpture, only to be topped by next year's ice dinosaurs. There will be castles made from chopped liver and scientifically designed kosher squid and shrimp made from recycled knishes, all served by ethnically correct waiters dressed in appropriate garb ranging from the sheepskin capes of Serbo-Croatian terrorists to Eskimos in frozen mukluks. And the price of this phantasmagoria of food is . . . one tuxedo, reasonably well-fitting.

At the dinner seats are assigned to particular people who buy tickets ranging up to five thousand dollars each, and the waiters are instructed not to serve until they collect a ticket— not to mention that you may have taken a seat at a table purchased by a Pakistani family who may not appreciate your explanation that you are Grandpa Abdul's illegitimate son—but the great food is at the reception. As long as you are wearing a tuxedo and saunter in with the assurance of John Wayne walking through the swinging doors of the Dodge City saloon, no one will question you. You can work your way from buffet table to buffet table, from girl to girl (or boy to boy, or a little of each, whatever your proclivity might be) without the slightest discomfort. If anyone suggests that they will meet you inside at the main dinner, put on your best Noël Coward sneer and say, "My dear boy, I have four other dinners to go to this evening."

PICKPOCKETS

Unless it gives them intense sexual pleasure, most normal people do not like somebody else's hand in their pockets, particularly if that hand is on a mission to grab their wallets, pocketbooks, or loose change. Since pickpockets have been around since toga times—and even received mention in the Bible—and are so prevalant that they probably stand a good chance of getting *their* pockets picked after they pick yours, there is no way to avoid them unless you go to a nudists' convention. There are, however, ways to defeat them or, at least, give their nimble fingers a run for their or, rather, *your* money. For example:

1. Never carry a knapsack with anything more than your dirty underwear in it. Knapsacks were invented by pickpockets. Putting anything of value in a knapsack is like putting valuables in the unlocked trunk of a car without a rearview mirror. Leave the knapsacks to soldiers. They don't have to worry about the soldier behind them, unless, of course, they are taking a shower.

2. Your brother-in-law and wife know exactly how you carry your money, but they have the decency to wait until you are asleep to put their hands in your pockets. Pickpockets, unless

they are your brother-in-law or wife, have to work on the law of averages. They assume that if you are a woman your money is in your pocketbook, and if you are a man, your wallet is in your rear trouser pocket. Therefore, women should always hold their pocketbooks under their arms or with their hands over the clasp. Men should keep their wallets in the inside breast pockets of their jackets or, if not wearing jackets, in their side trousers pockets.

3. Never look up at the tall buildings. Standing around looking up at the skyscrapers and comparing them to the skyline of Peoria is a hallmark of tourists. All over New York there are hordes of tourists from Peoria walking around with their heads up followed by armies of pickpockets with their heads down and their hands in the tourists' pockets.

4. Never wear short pants or white shoes. These are the uniforms of tourists. Nobody should *want* to look like a tourist unless they are out shopping for a case of gonorrhea to bring back to Peoria. Street prostitutes happily supply this to out-of-town visitors at special tourist rates. Pickpockets also love tourists more than the New York City Convention and Visitors Bureau. They know that tourists often walk around with all their money and credit cards on their persons, and even when they realize they are being or have just been robbed are so busy looking for a policeman on a horse or are too embarrassed to shout out that the pickpocket, even if spotted, has an excellent chance of making his escape.

5. Never be distracted. Pickpockets often work in pairs, since no pickpocket is adept enough to take your money or wallet out of your pocket without your being aware of what is going on unless you are, to a greater or lesser degree, distracted. One criminal does the distracting while the other picks your pocket.

Your suspicion level should rise if anything extraordinary occurs while you are taking a stroll. Any medical emergency not involving the spilling of blood (since few pickpockets are devoted enough to bleed a little in order to steal your wallet) should alert you to a possible danger of being pickpocketed. If you see someone writhing on the street, frothing at the mouth, reaching out to you for help, help if that is your proclivity but keep your hand on your wallet. If you feel your body brushed against, rubbed, or otherwise manhandled, reach for your wallet, unless it is a beautiful blonde doing the brushing or rubbing. If it is a beautiful blonde, reach for whatever you can grab.

More Short Takes

BEDS

In the City of New York if you can't get the desired body to fit your bed, at least you can get the desired bed to fit your body.

Dixie Foam (104 West 17th Street). If you don't mind sleeping on foam (which is basically bubbles—and the only Bubbles we could imagine sleeping on was a stripper who opened for the comics in Union City) and particularly if you actually enjoy sleeping on foam, this is the best place in New York. Foam costs less than regular mattresses or box springs and comes in at least a dozen grades of density. On the best of the foam beds there is a fifteen-year warranty. An added benefit is that if you get thrown out of your house you can just roll up your bed and move into your girlfriend's apartment.

Kleinsleep. Kleinsleep has three stores in Manhattan and seventeen other locations in the New York area. You can buy mattresses, box springs, headboards, daybeds, and frames. The prices are low and Kleinsleep offers free delivery if you insist upon it. Their downtown clearance center, where floor samples and discounted or discontinued models end up, recently has been banished to Patchogue, Long Island. You can get a terrific buy on a $400 mattress, but it will cost you another $10,000 to crate it back to New York City.

Sleepy's, the Mattress Professionals. Sleepy's is New York's biggest chain of mattress stores, often offering the lowest prices in town. Particularly watch for sale dates.

BOOKS

Barnes & Noble. Barnes & Noble generally offers a 10 percent discount on new books and sometimes more. The stores are excellent places to meet a prospective mate. Simply pick the category that interests you: photography, dance, sadomasochism, etc. Stand in front of the bookshelf and you may find someone with the same interest and take them home along with the book. Barnes & Noble used to have a spectacular sales annex on lower Fifth Avenue. Since that outlet closed, the branches around the City have been setting up tables for drastically discounted remainders, warehouse clearance items, reviewers' copies, and damaged books.

The Strand Bookstore (828 Broadway). Books, books, books piled in every conceivable corner of this huge old falling-apart store. There is a basement and side rooms. It looks old, dusty, and dirty and smells the same way, but you can literally find a book on any topic. Furthermore, if you call up they will locate a book if it is in stock and will hold it for four days. Downstairs they have a damaged book section. This is bargain browser's heaven. They even have a rare book collection and a first edition collection, but they are only available weekdays and usually one must call in advance.

CDs, RECORDS, TAPES, AND VIDEOS

J & R (23–33 Park Row). J & R is its own world, with one store after another side by side. There is J & R computer world, camera outlet, music world, jazz outlet, budget music, and video outlet. Everything is steeply discounted, and if you're moving into a new apartment and have nothing but your underwear, you can start at the first store and end up down the block with a fully electronically and musically equipped household, including telephones, computers, video machines and tapes, CDs, stereo, fax machine, juicer, blender, vacuum cleaner, and microwave. The only thing they do not supply is a girl to clean up after you and cook. They also have an efficient repair department in the basement and are one of the few shops in New York City that can repair what they sell you.

Footlight Records (113 East 12th Street). This store stocks mostly vinyl records with a specialty in show tunes and movie soundtracks. This is particularly good if you have an old phonograph, and even better if you have old ears. Here you can find records that are not available elsewhere.

Second Hand Rose's Sixth Avenue Shop (525 Sixth Avenue). This store also specializes in vinyl, but it has an emphasis on jazz, also soul, R&B, oldies, etc. Prices are moderate.

Tower Records Clearance Outlet (20 East 4th Street). Tower has the lowest prices in town. The merchandise consists of overstocks and cutouts in everything from classical to grunge rock, on records, cassettes, CDs and videotapes. They are loaded with tons of previously viewed movies and black-and-white film classics.

FURNITURE AND FURNISHINGS

If you are not a build-it-yourself person (and not many people have built themselves) and therefore cannot go to Ikea in New Jersey, there is a little known secret about how to order furniture directly from the manufacturers. In North Carolina they do not eat, drink, or play mahjong. They do nothing but manufacture furniture as they're coming and going from the trailer parks.

You should begin by going to furniture stores in New York to examine the merchandise and any catalogues available. Carefully write down the manufacturer and model numbers for the pieces in which you are interested. Then you can order the model by number directly from the manufacturer. You save up to 50% of the cost of the furniture by dealing directly with North Carolina, wherever it may be. Some people even fly down to North Carolina and spend a weekend shopping then return with their home completely furnished. Two of the largest galleries are Rose (919-886-6050) and Windsor (919-883-9000). These two galleries represent over one hundred different manufacturers.

Williams-Sonoma Outlet Center (231 Tenth Avenue). This is a closeout center for four different stores: Williams-Sonoma, Gardeners Eden, Pottery Barn, and Hold Everything. You can save all of your catalogue shopping for this place where everything is deeply discounted. The stock changes constantly, so repeat visits could be fruitful.

Fishs Eddy (889 Broadway). The final resting place for china from hotels and restaurants that have gone out of business, country clubs that are overstuffed, and manufacturers that have made extra pieces for themselves when there are specialty orders. There are some pieces going back twenty and thirty years or more. Genghis Khan's dinner service for eight was recently on sale. It is worth a browse for a bargain.

Broadway Panhandler (477 Broome St.). A huge selection of pots, pans, knives, serving pieces, and every kind of gadget imaginable for the kitchen. If your girlfriend says, "peel me a grape," you can reach into your drawer now and do it in a minute.

The Bowery (north and south of Canal Street). This is the restaurant supply center of New York. Restaurant-grade utensils are more sturdy and more functional than those sold in the chichi yuppie kitchenware stores. If you want to make pancakes for two thousand people or need a deep fat fryer to make your husband well done, this is the place to go.

COFFEE AND TEA

Porto Rico Importing Company (201 Bleecker Street). If you don't want to go to Starbucks and pay five dollars for café au lait, sit on a small stool that you can't fit on, have to carry your own coffee to the stool, and then be expected to leave a tip, go to Porto Rico. Here there are sacks and sacks of top quality coffee beans from all over the world deeply discounted to an average of $4.99 a pound. The staff is gracious and knowledgeable. They will grind the beans and will ship them anywhere. They also sell a wide variety of teas, coffee pots, and condiments.

Ten Ren Tea & Ginseng Company (75 Mott Street). Visiting this tea shop is like stepping back in time. Ten Ren grows its tea in Asia and then imports it here. There is a tremendous variety of inexpensive loose teas, teas in bags, and even a daily tea ceremony in which you can participate upon request. The staff is willing and will explain the differences among the teas and let you taste them, and they will teach you how to brew them. If someone says that you don't even know how to boil water, you can say, "Maybe so, but I know how to brew tea."

DELICACIES

Fairway (2328 Twelfth Avenue). This is an amazingly huge store, but you have to have a Sherman tank to get through the neighborhood safely and have someone waiting in the car for a quick getaway. All kinds of groceries are sold discounted and in normal or huge quantity. There is cooked food and baked goods, as well as all the usual supermarket items, all under one roof. They even have insulated coats for the customers to enter the cold food department where they sell fish, meat, dairy, etc. The store has now become a regular meeting place in New York.

Caviar-Polarica (73 Hudson Street). Sevruga or osetra goes for around one hundred dollars for a seven-ounce tin. While this may seem a lot for dead fish eggs, this is about the lowest you will find in New York, and the store will deliver free of charge.

Zito Bakery (259 Bleecker). The scent of Italian bread in the ovens beneath the store wafting up the sidewalks of Bleecker Street every morning is enough to add five pounds and four hundred calories.

Murray's Cheese Store (257 Bleecker). To go with the bread from Zito's you can pick up a hunk of Parmesan or any other cheese, and then in the neighborhood pick up fresh pasta and sauce at *Tutta Pasta (26 Carmine Street)*.

H & H Bagels (639 West 46th Street) **and Tal Bagels** (979 First Avenue).

Russ & Daughters (179 East Houston Street). Eating bagels without lox is like marrying a girl who has no money. For the best lox in town and also its fancier relatives, Norwegian and smoked salmon, go here.

. . . .

Taxis

. . . .

Forget all the ugly things you have heard about the New York taxi situation. Taxis in New York present absolutely no problem to a prospective passenger—that is, unless the passenger wants to go somewhere in one of them.

To a passenger, the problem falls into two categories. The first is finding a cab. The second is getting the cab to go where you want to go.

FINDING A CAB

Eleven o'clock on a sunny spring morning, if you hold up your hand to hail a taxi, cabs will cut one another off, go from one side of the street to the other, twist and swerve, dodge traffic and pedestrians, and converge on you with a fervor Eliot Ness reserved for pouncing on a load of bootleg hooch. *But* if it's rush hour or if a drop of rain has fallen or if people are merely asking, "Do you think it's *going* to rain?" taxis will be more scarce than Presbyterian ministers at a nudists' convention. Even if you spot an empty cab, forget it. Nothing—not sex, not winning the lottery, not a pastrami sandwich, not even buying wholesale—will bring more pleasure to a cabdriver's twisted heart than passing a fare by in the rain. Therefore, to be successful, you have to accept the fact that amateur night must be over. Getting a cab under these circumstances is now a game for the professionals.

The *Wither-Thou-Goest, I-Goest* Ploy

It unexpectedly begins to rain. Nobody is prepared for it, since everyone had listened to the weathercaster predicting that the weather at the airport would be clear and sunny. Unfortunately, none of the people you are standing with, holding soggy newspapers over their heads, lives at the airport, so you have all been caught totally unprepared by the sudden cloudburst.

A taxi cruises slowly down the street, driven by a refugee camel driver from Bombay with a demonic grin on his face. Anybody who thinks sex is the most fun a person can have without laughing out loud never met an Indian cabdriver who has had an opportunity to pass up a prospective passenger in the rain. Indeed, this idea brings such joy to the Indian community in New York that it goes on an alert when rain is predicted. Hordes of Indian taxi drivers are prepared to be dispatched at the first sign of precipitation in order to pass up Jewish businessmen who hail them.

Once cabbies have had their fill of passing up sodden fares, they then become uptown/downtown specialists. The cabbie decides where *he* wants to be at the end of his shift—whenever that might be—and only takes fares going in *his* general direction. Nonetheless, a cab will remain empty when it is raining or during rush hour for about as long as it takes to lick a stamp.

When you do spot that rarest of all gas-eating creatures, an empty cab with a driver on duty, it is for one of two possible reasons. The first possibility is that the cabbie has, at that very moment, dropped off a fare and you just have been lucky enough, out of all the hordes of people waiting for cabs, to be standing in *exactly* the right spot at the *exact* time the prior passenger left the cab. The odds of this happening are about the same as seeing the pope do a tap dance routine at the Apollo Theater's amateur night.

The second possibility is far more likely: the cabdriver spotted a fare, stopped, but before the prospective passenger could open the door, the cabbie asked the customer where he or she wanted to go. Clearly it was in a direction the driver did *not* want to go, and he told the fare where *he* could go. Except he would probably do so in New York "cabese:" "I'm just headed in for the night" (even if it's eleven o'clock in the morning), or "I have a flat tire and I'm headed for a garage" (It's *not* flat? So what. It may *become* flat). More imaginatively: "I just went through an area of high asbestos and am on my way to a decontamination chamber," or "I have bubonic plague that I picked up in Pakistan, but if you have had all of your vaccinations, there is no problem." He may explain that he is in the midst of an Indian ritual of self-abuse and will be finished in about three minutes, but you should wait outside until he finishes because he would like a little privacy. Or he may simply snap the door locks down, cursing you in any one of a thousand Indian dialects as he roars off with your hand poised midway in the air about to grab the door handle.

When you see a cab with its light on, what you must do is point your finger in whatever direction the cab is going. The cabdriver will instantly recognize you are a sophisticated taxi rider who understands that with the falling of a drop of rain he becomes the master and you the slave. Jump in the cab, and after you are seated, keep pointing in his chosen direction as you unintelligibly mumble your real destination. Once the cab is moving, and the meter starts running, tell him in simple English (in spite of what you may have heard, the odds are in your favor that this is a language with which he has at least a passing familiarity), where you really want to go. He is now obligated by law to take you to your destination.

If he refuses, don't budge from the seat and tell him to take you to the nearest police station or to stop by the nearest police officer. Asking a policeman to force the driver to take you where you want to go will have the same success rate as trying to sell the man in blue a ticket to the fireman's ball. The reason the cop cannot clap the cuffs on the Pakistani pirate is because, unfortunately, under the law a police officer can do no more than advise you how to file a complaint against the cabdriver. However, since your driver is probably an illegal immigrant who would sooner visit his proctologist than a police station, he most often will decide taking you where you want to go is a more pleasant alternative.

The cop will usually try to convince the cabbie to take you to your requested destination, however, in the interests of international harmony. One thing the cop will *not* do is to tell you to get out of the cab. This places your driver in the unenviable position of having to choose between spending the rest of his natural life with you in the backseat of his cab or delivering you to your destination. As a practical proposition probably the worst he can do to you is give you a few blasts of curry breath as he takes you where you want to go.

The *It's-Every-Man-for-Himself,* or *No-More-Mr.-Nice-Guy* Maneuver

The best physical preparation for getting a taxi during rush hour is training as a linebacker with the Washington Redskins. You will also have to be prepared mentally and emotionally. You must forget fair play, politeness, etiquette, and sportsmanship. All of these Christian virtues will leave you standing in the rain with packages in each arm while other people snicker at you from passing cabs. They will have won: you will have lost. They will think you are from New Jersey. You will feel like it.

On the average busy New York street at rush hour, or at any time if it is raining, there are half a dozen people lined up along the block desperately looking in the same direction for any empty cab coming their way. There will always be people ahead of you ready to pounce on the first vacant cab unless you are standing outside the taxi garage. It is hardly likely that you would be standing outside a taxi garage, since they are all located in neighborhoods with girls standing outside who all have the same telephone number: 1-900-MATTRESS.

The first thing you must do is develop a positive mind-set. You must convince yourself that no matter what is required of you, you *will* get the taxi. For you this task must become the moral equivalent of getting the last train out of Paris before the occupation, the last helicopter out of Saigon, or the last trolley car out of Pompeii before Mount Vesuvius got the hiccups. You must tell yourself that you *will* get ahead of the person waiting down the block for the next empty cab. And you must do just that.

Start strolling down the block past these people in the direction of where the cab will come. Act innocent. Pretend to be a student of urban architecture examining the buildings, curbs, etc. Another ploy is to pretend to be lost, checking street numbers and signs. The point is to really be keeping an eye down the street, looking for the next cab, while at the same time not alerting your competition to the fact that you are a player. When an empty cab pulls up ahead of you for the fare, you must spring into action. Sprinting forward, running around and between pedestrians and cars, jump ahead of the passenger about to enter the cab and mumble about being "in a family way." Of course, if you are a man this excuse will not convince anybody. In that case, shout out that you are a physicist and there is a runaway atomic chain reaction in Pittsburgh heading east needing your immediate attention. You must stop off at home to pick up your toothbrush, since it is a custom of physicists to never go to a chain reaction without first brushing their teeth.

If you are a woman and the cabdriver has the nerve to ask you, as you settle back in your seat, how far gone in your pregnancy you are (or the Bangladesh equivalent), tell him "Twenty minutes," and add that you are very tired.

CHANGE

There are only three things a cabdriver needs to begin his working day: a taxi, gas (for the car, not what he gets from his breakfast of soft-boiled curry), and change. Figuring that two out of three is not so bad, no cabbie will admit he starts the day with enough silver and small bills to give you change for anything over a nickel.

Some legitimately start the day with no change because they don't want to affect the cut of their carefully tailored outfit, consisting in the summer of khaki shorts over hairy legs and in the winter of layers of unwashed smelly woolen sweaters over a body in a similar condition. Others feel they don't need change because in the course of the day "Allah will provide." Hopefully, Allah can get a favorable exchange rate on rupees from Jewish bankers notwithstanding his disciples blowing up a few buses here and there in Israel.

The truth is most cabbies have so much change in their pockets that if they went through a metal detector, they would drag it down the street after them. The reason they profess to have no change is because in their quasi-criminal cunning they reason that if they say they have no change, in your haste to get on with your business as you leave the taxi you will simply say, "Keep the change." Your remedy is very simple. When arriving at your destination, as long as you have given the Bombay bandit a twenty-dollar bill or smaller, the law says it is *his* problem, not yours. Therefore, smile sweetly and say, "Sorry, this is the smallest I have." He will either have to accept whatever money you give him and waive the unpaid balance and/ or tip or obtain change for you by reaching into one of the mysterious crevices under the seat or dashboard. Even if you do not have anything under a twenty-dollar bill you have committed no crime, and there is nothing the cabdriver can do except get out and stop other cabbies to obtain change.

Some drivers may legitimately have no change and so inform you of this fact as you enter the cab. It is between you and your conscience whether you say, "Don't worry," and then after you get to your destination explain to the cabbie that when you said, "Don't worry," you were not talking about your ability to pay and not require change, but rather, you were talking about the smell in the car and that you seem to be immune.

YOUR RIGHTS

The Bill of Rights that comes with the Constitution is good enough to protect the rights of citizens all across the country and serve as a model for the rest of the world. However, since it was not as difficult back then for Thomas Jefferson to hail a cab during rush hour as it would be for him to do it today— not to mention that all the cabbies in those days spoke English and could take you to Bloomingdale's without stopping fourteen times to ask directions—the city has issued a special ten-point "Taxi Rider's Bill of Rights."

As a Taxi Rider, You Have the Right to:
1. Direct the Destination and Route Used
You certainly can tell the driver where you want to go since

that is the whole point of getting into the cab in the first place, unless you simply enjoy sitting on a dirty plastic-covered seat or are a student of the Kashmiri fertility chants playing on the cabbie's radio. Telling him how to get there, on the questionable assumption that he understands what you are saying, is quite another matter. If he truly knows how to get to your destination, his natural inclination will be to go there by way of downtown Anchorage. If he does not know how to get where you want to go, you are in for a ride with screaming conversations in Hindustani over his radio, interspersed with, if you listen carefully, several "Jew bastids," and stops, at your expense as the meter ticks on, to ask directions every few blocks.

Your best approach, if you are going any place more obscure than the Empire State Building, is to find out the directions beforehand, and then give them to the driver when you get in the cab in simple four-letter words. He will tell you that there was just a watermain break on one of the streets you want to go down and his sister-in-law told him there is a Ku Klux Klan rally going on in another street of your choice. Tell him politely that you wanted to wash your feet anyway and that you love the chopped liver they serve at Klan rallies. The inescapable point is, his sister-in-law notwithstanding, you want him to go *your* way. He has no choice but to follow your directions.

2. Go to Any Destination in the Five Boroughs

Generally if you get into a cab in Manhattan and ask to be taken to Brooklyn or, God forbid, Staten Island, the driver will look at you as if you asked him to take you to Mount Rushmore. It is very clear, however, that until Brooklyn or Staten Island secede from New York, they are still part of the city, and the driver has no choice but to honor your request. But unless you have specific directions to get to your destination, your ride will be reminiscent of Balboa trying to find a route to the Pacific. There are also parts of Brooklyn, Queens, and the Bronx that are more dangerous than the jungles through which Balboa beat his path. It is not uncustomary for people who live in the outer boroughs to give Xeroxed copies of directions and sometimes a small map explaining how to get to their homes.

If the driver agrees to take you to Westchester or Nassau counties, the fare is the metered amount to the city limits, plus twice the metered amount from city limits to destination, plus round-trip tolls. Kennedy Airport from Manhattan is, as of this writing, a flat thirty-dollar charge. If you want to go to Newark Airport the fare is the metered amount, plus ten dollars, plus the round-trip tolls. If you want to go to any other point outside the city, the driver has the right to agree or refuse to take you. If he will take you, the fare must be agreed upon *before* starting the trip.

3. A Courteous, English-Speaking Driver Who Knows the Streets in Manhattan and the Way to Major Destinations in Other Boroughs

This article of the Bill of Rights contains four requirements. If you ever find a driver who possesses all of these virtues, not only would he qualify for the Golden Apple Award, the Oscar, Tony, and Emmy—not to mention a mayoralty proclamation and a ticker tape parade—but you should immediately have him cloned and shipped to Jurassic Park, so rare is this creature.

4. A Driver Who Knows and Obeys All Traffic Laws

There are two inexorable truths about New York traffic laws. The first is that virtually nobody can understand them fully. Streets are replete with signs indicating you can make a left turn only from 4 P.M. to 7 P.M. except in the summer when it is 4 P.M. to 9 P.M. Saturday and Sunday but not from the bus lane but okay from the snow removal lane provided you are not in the bicycle lane during business hours except on religious holidays. As a result of this, there are scores of Jews and visitors from Kansas City who have been driving around and around the island of Manhattan since last Thanksgiving trying to figure out when they can make a left turn. Every time they ask a cop if they can make the turn, the answer is always the same: "Can't you read the sign?"

The second inexorable truth is, if your driver obeys all the traffic rules, especially during rush hour, you will have to consult a calendar rather than your watch to see when you will arrive at your destination. If, however, you see that you have a cab-driver who is looking to qualify for the Indianapolis 500, or if you find yourself clutching his rosary or composing your last will and testament while he practices fighter plane tactics with the taxi, no amount of instruction will change his basic nature. The best bet is to bail out at the next stoplight and say a quick prayer for the next passenger.

5. Air-Conditioning on Demand

One of the great achievements of the twentieth century is air-conditioning—ranking up there with the discovery of penicillin and the Hula Hoop. The last place you would think it necessary would be in a moving vehicle. But the first place it is needed is in a New York taxi, condemned by the largest traffic problem in the world to operate in two speeds: "stopped" and "inch along." Couple this unfortunate situation with being entombed in the same hot metal capsule with a driver who is a member of the Gaavatarbaluvita sect of the upper Kuwalakundi Valley whose religious beliefs preclude bathing in any month during which soap is sold and is in the midst of breaking the fast of Ramadan by imbibing a curry cocktail. Although even Amnesty International would require air-conditioning, the problem was that since air-conditioning an automobile uses up extra gasoline and the drivers themselves come from countries where they use their fathers' bald heads to fry eggs in the summer, anytime a passenger asks for air-conditioning he is automatically told that the unit is broken. In the unlikely event the driver came from a country north of the thirty-eighth parallel and the air-conditioning was turned on, the partition between driver and passenger would effectively prevent the air-conditioning from reaching the backseat. To add insult to discomfort, in perfect cabdriver logic, if a passenger gasping for fresh, albeit warm, air was bold enough to open a window hoping to let in some air, he would be met with a terse, "Don't lower da window. Yer letting in de hot air."

In 1996, to the chagrin of the drivers and the delight of the passengers, Christopher Lynn, Mayor Giuliani's newly appointed taxi commissioner, mandated that all cabs be equipped with devices to transmit cool air back to the passenger section. Putting aside the unhappy fact that since the Third Reich, no Jew can feel quite comfortable in a closed space facing the collection of ventilated pipes and fans now being utilized for this purpose, and putting aside the rumors that along with the cool air being passed back to the passenger is an army of bacteria that would make Louis Pasteur get sexually excited, the fact is that Commissioner Lynn's directive now gives the cab rider a shot at a comfortable ride on a sweltering summer day.

Since most cab rides are of short duration, it is imperative to give the instruction to the driver to turn on the air-conditioning as soon as you enter the taxi. If air-conditioning is requested, a popular way for drivers to effectively circumvent the new rule is to turn it on at its lowest level. Therefore, one should look over the driver's shoulder to make sure the dial is set for the maximum air-conditioning and the highest fan setting. If not, this fact should be sweetly pointed out to the cabbie.

If cabbies are to be believed, taxi air conditioners have the highest breakdown rate of any invention of Western civilization. The next time the driver tells you the air conditioner is broken, tell him to turn it on anyway since you love hot air blowing on you or that you are a faith healer for air conditioners and are the best thing for an ailing air conditioner next to sending it on a trip to Lourdes.

6. A Radio-Free (Silent) Trip

For some inexplicable reason every cab has the radio speaker in *back* rather than in the front where the driver sits. Worse yet, the speaker is strategically placed behind the passenger's head and usually between the place where two passengers sit, thereby rendering conversation between passengers impossible. Therefore, when the rules call for the right to a "silent trip," until the driver is corrected, his view of the rule is that the "silent trip" applies to your lack of a right to converse with your companion.

The *good* news is that, upon request, the driver will, give or take a few mutterings and incantations of "May Allah make your unborn child come forth in the world with the deformed tusks of a syphilitic walrus," turn the radio off. The *bad* news is that he will continue to plot jihad in jabberwocky over the two-way radio with all his colleagues who are similarly torturing their passengers.

7. Smoke- and Incense-Free Air

The right to smoke- and incense-free air loses some of its attractiveness when the interior of the taxi is redolent with the odors of yesterday's lunch of guacamole and tandoori liver sandwiches and the only free gas in the car has already passed through the large intestine of the driver. This is not to mention the mechanical smells of oil, gasoline, and brake and coolant fluids emanating from the geriatric gasps of an overworked engine (the car's not the driver's). Added to these are the city smells of this morning's garbage and diesel truck fuel. But you *do* have the right not to smell smoke or incense and *can* demand the driver put out his cigarette or snuff out his incense—all of which has about the same practical effect as going to Coney Island and trying to use a bucket to empty out the Atlantic Ocean.

8. A Clean Passenger Seat Area

Clean compared to what? If the comparison is to the living room of a Baghdad brothel on a Sunday morning after the local bowling team had their Saturday night tryouts on a warm night, then the backseat could qualify for the *Good Housekeeping* seal of approval. Otherwise the seats laden with the remains of sticky soda and last night's romantic interludes cry out for the dispatching of a decontamination team from the Centers for Disease Control.

Unfortunately, there is, for all intents and purposes, nothing you can do about it. If you demand the driver clean the car, you face the prospect of standing outside the cab, wasting time, while watching the driver go through the third world version of spring cleaning. You can, of course, file a complaint against the driver but, as will be explained later, this exercise of good citizenship may cause you more discomfort than it does the cabbie.

9. A Clean Trunk

If the trunk were truly clean it would be a viable alternative to riding in the backseat. After all, lying back in the trunk you would have privacy, quiet, and not even have to look at the driver. However, in the real world a cabdriver's trunk is his repository for tools, tires he has to repair, rags, cleaning supplies, and dirty videotapes that he is hiding from his wife. But let us pose some sensible basic questions. What is it your business what

the cabdriver has in his trunk? Are you going to take your
family to it for a weekend visit? Are you planning to cater your
son's bar mitzvah there? Are you going to send your brother-
in-law to the trunk to spend his summer vacation? Of course
not. And certainly not if the cabdriver doesn't rent it to you at
a great price—better than wholesale. At least at cost. So why
not spend your energies worrying about *real* problems like who
you can sue if the garage *almost* scrapes your car or how much
you can take off your rent if the elevator in your apartment
building is broken for a day.

10. Refuse to Tip if the Above Are Not Complied With

This tenth item on the Taxi Rider's Bill of Rights is a perfect
example of why we should have stopped issuing bills of rights
after Thomas Jefferson got finished with his. When the taxi
bosses sat down they apparently decided that to have a Bill of
Rights with only nine rights sounded too chintzy. "Ten" sounded
like a better number so they added a tenth right. Now, do you
really have to have it written down that you have the right not
to tip if the driver does not do what he is supposed to? You
have the right not to tip even if he *does* everything exactly right.
You are never going to see the driver again. If you did, you
would not recognize him. He can't tell your wife about the
blonde you were with in the backseat. Not unless he ends up
in the backseat with your wife, and then you *certainly* don't have
to give him a tip. The reason you give him a tip is because you
are a decent person and . . . he stays away from your wife.

FARES

Taxi drivers are living repudiation of the first principle in geom-
etry that "the shortest distance between two points is a straight
line." Indeed, New York City cabbies have a finely honed

methodology of how to get from one place to another by the *longest* possible route. We have compiled, with the cooperation of the Taxi and Limousine Commission, sample fares between common destinations. These should serve as a guide to determine if your driver is "taking you for a ride," or at least not the ride you expected when you got into the cab.

Sample Fares from 57th Street & Fifth Avenue

Brooklyn Botanic Garden	$17.00 to $18.00
Chelsea Pier	$8.60
Chinatown (Canal St. & Mott St.)	$11.70
City Hall	$18.00
Empire State Bldg.	$4.70
Gracie Mansion	$6.20
Grand Central Terminal	$4.00
Greenwich Village	$8.70
Harlem (125th St.)	$18.40
Intrepid	$4.70
La Guardia Airport	$16.50
Newark Airport	$48.80
Pennsylvania Station	$6.20
Port Authority Bus Terminal	$5.30
Soho	up to $8.50
South Street Seaport	$12.10
Staten Island Ferry Terminal	$14.00
Stock Exchange/ Wall Street	$11.70
Theater district (44th & Broadway)	$4.40
2 World Trade Center	$12.00 to $13.00
Yankee Stadium	$18.00

The fare from JFK airport to any destination in Manhattan is $30.00, not including tolls or a tip. The TLC suggests a five dollar tip.

COMPLAINTS

After an unsuccessful run-in with a cabdriver, when everything you have tried to do by yourself to remedy the situation has failed and grumbling about the Nazi bastards, yelling at your wife, or a meaningful call to a 900 number gives you no emotional relief, you can always file a complaint with the Taxi and Limousine Commission.

To file a complaint call the TLC at 212-303-TAXI or write to them at 221 West 41st Street, New York, NY 10036 (Fax 212-840-1607), and a complaint form will be sent to you by mail. When writing back with the details of the complaint, as much of the following information as possible should be included:

the taxi's medallion number
the driver's name and license number
date, time, and location of the ride
your mailing address and daytime phone number

You will be notified of the date and time of the hearing. If the date set for the hearing is inconvenient for you, at least five business days before the scheduled date call 212-840-4572 and the date will be rearranged to suit you. If you don't show up, the complaint will be dismissed. If you harbor the thought that you will request a hearing intending not to show up but merely to inconvenience the driver, bear in mind that there are no such things as free lunches in life. You will ultimately pay for the needless administrative costs you have incurred by virtue of higher taxes and ultimately higher taxi fares, since all these things are ultimately factored into the city's expenses and the taxi company's cost of doing business. If the driver does not show up, he can be suspended or fined.

Both before and after the hearing every effort is made to avoid a face-to-face meeting with the driver who was unattractive enough when you only had to look at the back of his head. There is a separate waiting area for complainants, and an inspector is available to escort you out of the building after the hearing. So if the driver is putting pins in a doll that looks like you, at least you will not see it. But if, after the hearing, you get this sudden sticking pain in your side . . .

Used Cars

When you go out with a girl, do you pick the one who will cost the least on the first date or do you pick one who in the long run will cost you less money because you will not have to drag her broken-down body to plastic surgeons to pick up what has fallen down and whose teeth you will not have to replace six months after you marry her? You, because you are a schmuck—and a cheap one at that—will probably pick a girl who is a cheap date, looks good on the outside, and will probably give you a good ride until three months after you get married when she will start getting headaches or be too tired to come across.

The way schmucks date girls is the same way they buy used cars. The cheapest way to buy a used car is from a private party. You choose a car that looks good and drives around the block reasonably well, and you save all the overhead and profit that a car dealer builds into his price for an automobile. However, the elements of overhead the dealer must absorb are all things that, in the long run, are beneficial to you and suggest that a car dealer is the person from whom to purchase a used car.

There are two kinds of dealers who sell used cars. There are dealers who sell nothing but used cars, and there are new car dealers who sell used cars as an adjunct to their new car dealership. You can save yourself a trip to Atlantic City by buying a used car from a dealer selling only used cars. The odds of purchasing from a used car dealer a first-class car that will be serviced, maintained, and have any defect corrected by skilled mechanics are somewhere between your chances of winning at the slots and winning at Russian Roulette.

A used car dealer buys his cars at auction without, generally, even a road test or he buys them at bargain prices from some walk-in who is desperate for money or from an individual who has been stuck with some misbegotten product of the Industrial Revolution and who now wants to get rid of his misfortune and pass it on to somebody else. If it were another age, and this were a horse instead of a car, he would pull it up to the side of the road and shoot it to put it out of its misery. This is the car the used car dealer would like to polish up and pass off to you. As far as a mechanic is concerned, if he has one at all, and he can sober him up, the mechanic has probably learned his trade at the Sing Sing outreach program.

A new car dealer, whose primary business is not selling used cars, invariably is required by the manufacturer to maintain a staff of factory-trained mechanics and, as a car dealer, is regulated by state lemon laws.

We discussed the lemon law with Howard Koeppel of Koeppel Motors, who explained he invested and continues to invest hundreds and hundreds of thousands of dollars so he can comply with this law that is designed to protect consumers. A used car dealer, who doesn't have to comply, can put that money into devising new ways to bilk you. And a private individual who sells a car, Mr. Koeppel explains, is not covered by this law. Therefore, when you buy a car from your friendly neighbor and you later find when you raise the hood that it is powered by two Roman slaves chained together who are now hungry, you have none of the protections or remedies of the law.

THE LEMON LAW

Whether a vehicle is covered by the lemon law is governed by the age of the car, computed from the date of delivery, and the number of miles driven.

If the vehicle from the date of its original delivery has been driven 18,000 miles or less, the manufacturer's express warranty shall be honored up to the earlier of 18,000 miles or 24 months. The warranty must cover the seven items listed below.

If the vehicle has been driven more than 18,000 miles, but less than 36,000 miles, or is more than 24 months in service from the date of its delivery, the warranty shall be 90 days or 4,000 miles, whichever first occurs.

If the vehicle has been driven more than 30,000 miles, but less than 80,000 miles, the warranty shall be 60 days or 3,000 miles, whichever first occurs.

Over 80,000 miles, better buy a horse, and over 100,000 miles, the lemon law doesn't apply.

Once a vehicle falls under the protection of the lemon law, the following items are covered:

1. engine, all lubricated parts, water pump, fuel pump, manifolds, engine block, cylinder heads, rotary engine housings, and flywheels
2. transmissions, the transmission case, internal parts, and the torque converter
3. drive axle, front and rear drive axle housing and internal parts, axle shaft, propeller shafts, and universal joints

4. brakes, master cylinder, vacuum assist booster, wheel cylinder, hydraulic lines and fittings, and disc brake calipers
5. radiator
6. steering, steering gear housing and all internal parts, owner steering pump, valve body piston and rack
7. alternator, generator, and starter ignition system excluding battery.

Additionally, a new car dealership that as a sideline also sells used cars will intimately know its own brand of cars—old and new—and be able to spot a real or potential problem and most likely be in a position to deal with it expeditiously. Aside from wanting to preserve a good name in the neighborhood, for purely selfish economic reasons, new car dealers selling used cars don't want to have the car brought back to them, since their mechanics are paid approximately forty-five dollars or more an hour.

Many new car dealerships sell cars that they have taken in trade but that they consider to be substandard to the conventional used car lots. Therefore, if you purchase an automobile from a used car lot, you might be getting a car rejected by both its prior owner and a professional dealer. You might take a girl who is a double reject out for an evening of fun, but you would certainly be very careful before you got involved in a long-term relationship with her.

Lastly, here are a few other things that you can check by yourself before you buy a used car:
1. interior condition
2. oil pressure
3. electrical system
4. air-conditioning system/heating system
5. trunk interior—is it damp or wet?—if so, you have a leak

6. any leaks under the car
7. engine compression
8. car finish—original or repaint
9. signs of accidents
10. uneven tire wear
11. ownership history (was the car owned by a young person likely to drive it hard?)
12. original history of car (check the vehicle ID affixed to the engine and call the manufacturer, who will tell you the original history of the car)

There are also services, such as the "Lemon Detector," (718-643-2920). An individual will come to you with a van loaded with equipment and run a two-hundred-point check of the car. The "doctor" will look at everything from the trunk lock to the engine to the air conditioning, and will evaluate the worth of the car. His report will give you something with which to negotiate. However, if you get stuck with several duds in a row you can end up paying more than if you bought the car from a reputable dealer in the first place.

Words to Survive By

YIDDISH

Yiddish is not itself an accepted language in the family of languages. Starting with a German base, it is a cocktail of languages influenced by all the countries of eastern Europe through which Jews have journeyed on their sometimes fruitless quest for a permanent home. The language has been filtered through the kishkes (intestines or guts always belonging to a person who has undergone misery) of untold generations of suffering Jews. Since there are more Jews in New York than in any other city in the world, Yiddish, or at least select phrases of this dialect, have become part of almost every New Yorker's vocabulary. New York, however, has added the music of its streets to the self-mocking expressiveness of immigrants to craft a new version of the language.

Understanding key Yiddish phrases is vital to survival in New York. In New York, it is impossible not to be either coming from, going to, buying from, selling to, being treated by, benefitting from, being fleeced by, taken advantage of, complimented by, or cursed by a Jew. At the very least, without understanding a few Yiddish survival words, you will not understand what has happened, or is about to happen, to you.

Key Yiddish Survival Words and Phrases

Ahf Tsu Loches (pronounced *ahf-tsoo-LOKH-ess*). Since there are so many people in New York, lots of bad things can happen to a person at the hands of another. To a Jew who believes misery is his lot in life, it is more attractive to curse fate rather than the lowlife who caused the problem. The phrase means, "As fate would have it."

"Just my luck. I loan a friend all my money, and, *ahf tsu loches,* he opens a store across the street. He wipes me out with my own money."

"I'm loaded down with packages, trying to hail a cab in the rain. My umbrella starts to fall. A lovely young woman offers to help. She takes hold of the umbrella, then, *ahf tsu loches,* a cab pulls up and she hops in, taking my umbrella with her and leaving me splashed and soaked on the corner."

Billik (pronounced *BILL-ick*). A major preoccupation of Jews is buying merchandise. But just purchasing it is not enough. It must be purchased at a reduced price. It is therefore natural that in New York City, the shopping capital of the world, a phrase dealing with buying things becomes part of the language. *Billik* means "cheap" or "inexpensive" and usually refers to something on which you got a good price. A Jew's greatest fear is to pay full price on anything. So if it's *billik vi borscht*—"cheap as beet soup"—he's happy.

A yenta says, "I paid three hundred dollars for a dress."

Her friend says "Three hundred dollars! You paid too much!"

The first woman says, "But it sold for five hundred dollars."

The friend says, "Oh what a deal!" Now she's thrilled. A two hundred dollar savings. *Billik vi borscht!*

Jewish wives are always saving their husbands millions of dollars this way. The wives say they're making their husbands rich with all the money they save on bargains. Meanwhile, the husbands are so rich they're walking around the neighborhood with holes in their shoes.

Chozzer (pronounced KCHA-zer). *Chozzer* means "pig." But the word is used much more generally in Yiddish. It describes a guy who wants everything, whether it belongs to him or not, and wants a hundred times more than he's entitled to. There's a *chozzer* on every block in New York.

A *chozzer* sits in a restaurant and orders a chicken. He eats the whole thing, then calls the owner over and says, "This meal is terrible. I want something else." He tries to get another main dish to replace the one he has devoured. A normal person would take a bite, and if he didn't like it, then call the owner over. Not the *chozzer*. He waits to finish it first, then demands his money back.

The owner says, "If the chicken was no good, how come it's not on your plate? How did the chicken disappear? Did a sanitation truck come and pick it up? No! You ate it!"

The *chozzer* replies, "Who ate it? I didn't eat it! New York is a dangerous place. People will steal anything here! I don't know where the chicken went—I'm not a detective. All I know is I'm hungry. I want something to eat."

A *chozzer* has endless *chutzpah* (see below). His extreme greediness knows no bounds.

Chutzpah (pronounced *KCHOOTS-pah*). If one word could be used to describe the archetypical New Yorker, this is it.

Someone with *chutzpah* is brazen, brash, ballsy. You can't survive in New York without a little *chutzpah* (and the more, the better), although every merchant you deal with usually has too much.

You bring your best evening gown to the tailor to fix the hem. By mistake he shortens it and cuts off the excess. Now you have a minidress that can't be lengthened or worn. Not only does he refuse to pay for the dress he ruined, he has the *chutzpah* to charge you double for redesigning it.

Feh (pronounced *feh!*). New York is a city where everybody is in a hurry even though they may have nowhere to go. They may push and shove people out of the way in subways and elevators and make believe they are late for a brain surgery operation, while the only place they are really going is to a park to pick up yesterday's newspaper. New York is a city where people in a rush talk in shorthand.

Feh is the shortest, most efficient, most undiplomatic, clearest, and fastest way to say in Yiddish "Boy, does that smell!" It is always used in the negative sense. You can say it about everything from a leftover herring to a dress for the opera to a politician's explanation for a tax increase.

Fumfer (pronounced *FOOM-fehr*). This is someone who can't or won't talk straight. He double-talks, he mumbles, he's tongue-tied. It could be that he has a mental block about the words or he's nervous or he's lying and can't extract the words the way he had planned.

You catch a pickpocket with his hand on your wallet. You shout, "Hey, what's your hand doing in my pocket?"

The thief is in a panic and talks so fast that he doesn't make any sense. " I thought it was *my* pocket. You're so close to me. How should I know it was your pocket? There's a lot of pockets on this bus. How am I supposed to know which one is mine?"

He chokes and gargles like he's got a bagel caught in his throat. He's called a *fumfer*.

Goy (pronounced like "Roy" with a G). If you don't know what a *goy* is, you aren't a New Yorker. Any gentile is a goy. The plural is *goyim*. Insecure goyim believe it is a term of condescension. This is absolutely inaccurate, except if you are talking about clothes, food, or jewelry. The truth is that the word has nothing to do with the quality or character of a person. It is strictly an identifying term. Sometimes, in jest, it is used derisively by *both* Jews and gentiles. They use it to poke fun at themselves when they say or do something not particularly shrewd. They will refer to themselves as having a *"goyisheh kop,"* a "gentile head." "What can you do? I've got a *goyisheh kop?"*

Handle (pronounced *HON-dle*). You absolutely cannot survive in New York if you can't *handle*. To *handle* is to bargain, to negotiate, or to work out a deal. A Jew isn't a Jew and a New Yorker isn't a New Yorker unless he can *handle*. *Handling* is not something to be taken casually. It has to be a way of life and something a person believes in like square dancing or white supremacy.

When a Jew comes home from buying something, there are always two questions: "What did they ask?" and "What did you pay?" If the storekeeper asked three hundred dollars and you paid anything close to that, you are considered a dummy and a failure because the most you should have paid was eighty dollars.

New Yorkers never feel cheap by *handling*: it is a tradition to *handle*. In small stores if you buy something without *handling* the store owner will probably make fun of you after you leave. What you do not know is that even in large department stores you can *handle* on expensive items. If an item is really expensive, ask to speak to the buyer for that particular department. Explain to him or her that you are a frequent customer of the store and would like to purchase the item, but the price is too high. Often you will receive a substantial reduction. Sometimes, the buyer will tell you a reduced price is not possible but will take your telephone number and will call you when it goes on sale.

Kishkes (pronounced *KISH-kees*). Your *kishkes* are what gets bounced around every time you take a cab ride. Literally translated, it's the guts or intestines. Figuratively speaking, it's when something touches your inner soul very deeply and profoundly. Like when your ex-wife unexpectedly calls you and tells you to stop sending her alimony because she doesn't feel comfortable, after twelve years, taking any more money, especially since you were only married for two hours before she sued you for divorce.

Mensch or Mench (rhymes with "clench"). *Mensch* literally means "person," a human being, but the broader meaning is a human being with class, with feelings, and with a sense of humanity. A *mensch* is a gentleman. A good *mensch* is hard to find in New York and, according to a young wives' tale, a hard *mensch* is good to find.

Anytime someone wants to give the ultimate compliment, he will say, "What a *mensch*." Everybody in New York wants to tell everybody else off. A *mensch* is someone who has the opportunity to tell you off but says nothing. If you find someone like this in New York, don't let him slip away.

Oy Vey (rhymes with "boy day"). *Oy vey* means "my God!" It also is: "How do you like that!" "I can't believe it!" "It's impossible!" "I don't know what's going to happen to me!" "It's all over for me!"

Oy vey is the ultimate Jewish expression. It encompasses

every negative feeling a Jew ever had. Anytime you feel rejected, disgusted, overwhelmed, miserable, bitter, *oy vey* covers it. Whatever the misery is, the first reaction is always *oy vey*.

You just found out the stock market crashed or that your wife is cheating or a hammer fell on your foot or you discover you forgot to pay your medical insurance and it lapsed or there is only one cuff link in the drawer or you missed the plane— the first thing a Jew says is always *oy vey*. No other phrase can describe your predicament better. All over New York the *oy veys* are colliding in the atmosphere.

Schlemiel and Schlimazel (pronounced *shleh-MEEL* and *SHLEH-MAH-zel*). These two go hand in hand. There's a common definition that a *schlemiel* is someone who spills soup on people, and a *schlimazel* is someone who gets soup spilled on him. The truth is, a *schlimiel* and a *schlemazel* are the same person. Usually they go out together. Each term is another way of saying someone is a jerk, an idiot, a screwball, a helpless individual.

As soon as a *schlemiel* gets on a bus the driver goes on strike. He's the guy who boards an airplane wanting to go to Oakland, California, and ends up in Auckland, New Zealand.

Guys like this are all over New York. Don't stand too close or get too friendly with them if you want to avoid the debris flying all around them.

Schlock (rhymes with "flock"). You can't shop in New York if you don't know this word. *Schlock* is junk; it's low class; it's garbage. A street vendor tries to sell you a fake leather fake Gucci bag. You take one look and say *"Feh! It's schlock."* It is all around you in New York. But you need Jewish radar to recognize *schlock* when you see it. Otherwise, your house will look like a museum of the rejects from Gimbel's basement.

Schmear (rhymes with "beer"). *Schmear* is a critical word. It can get you a seat in a crowded restaurant and you can also eat it. First of all, never ask for cream cheese on your bagel. Ask for a *schmear*. It's just what it sounds like: a *schmear*-smear of cream cheese on top of the bagel. It is also a payoff, a bribe. You can't get a reservation at a popular new restaurant, but you show up anyway. Every table is booked. They can't fit another table, chair, skinny gentile, or toothpick in the room. So you give the maître d' a *schmear*—kind of like cream cheese in the palm—and suddenly out of nowhere, a table appears. Just make sure you understand the meaning of a word before you use it and don't get the two meanings mixed up.

Schmuck (rhymes with "duck"). If you only know one survival word in Yiddish, know this one. When you use it, everyone will know what you mean. Actually, most people don't know the literal meaning of the word *schmuck*. They usually use it as the equivalent of "jerk," but the word comes from the German word for jewel. Jewels by their very nature are not large. Since Jewish men, anecdotally, are not known for the size of their private parts, although they still have a certain affection for them, it is easy to see how the word acquired a secondary meaning, and became a slang word for the male private parts. So when you call someone a *schmuck,* he's actually being called a penis, or *putz,* which is the Yiddish slang for *schmuck.*

If a man does anything to irritate, anger, annoy, or bother you can call him a *schmuck*. And New York is full of them.

Shmatte (pronounced *SHMOT-ta*). *Shmatte*, "rag," is a word that is basically an insult. If a woman is talking about what another woman is wearing, it's a *shmatte*. However, if she happens to own the same dress, it's "couture." In the context of clothing *shmatte* and *schlock* go together.

New York is the fashion capital of the world. So you should know that if you're walking around in something that doesn't have a designer label, you're wearing a *shmatte*. Women in New York don't talk about clothes, they talk about labels. My Saint Laurent and your Givenchy. Real New York women wear their labels on the *outside* of their dresses.

Jewish Foods

There are certain Jewish foods that are etched into the taste buds, if not the genetic memory, of every New Yorker. Not only have the recipes for these ethnic culinary masterpieces been preserved from generation to generation, but these dishes have also preserved their original names. This can be said of foods enjoyed by other ethnic groups in the city. However, no other group has been able to preserve the integrity of the composition and method of preparation of their dishes for as long as the Jewish people; no other group has been able to have so many of its dishes pass into the gastronomic vocabulary of the city. No language permits the literal translation of the name of the dish to be a shorthand description of the food to the degree that Yiddish does. In no other language does simply speaking the very name of the dish create a musical image of the dish. Without a short tour of Yiddish eating, your stomach will never know New York.

Chicken Soup (pronounced like it looks and tastes). *Chicken soup* is one of the hallmarks of being a Jewish New Yorker, or at least a person in New York who thinks Jewish. It is the all-purpose medicine, intestinal cleanser, and expression of friendship. When you're sick, you call Second Avenue Deli and have them send over a Chicken in a Pot—chicken soup with noodles, vegetables, and matzoh balls. Nothing can make you feel better faster.

Chicken soup has been a mainstay of the Jewish diet since the old days when poor Jews ate *chicken soup* in the bowl with potatoes on the side. Into the broth they would add a matzoh ball, some noodles, a kreplach (rolled dough with chopped meat inside) and have a whole meal. So between the potatoes and the *chicken soup,* the poverty-stricken Jew from the Lower East Side for thirty years was able to fill himself up for twenty cents a meal. Then the Jews left for the suburbs and turned their backs on lowly *chicken soup.* Now, when pasta became the biggest hit in American cuisine, the Jews didn't know it, but they were back to *chicken soup* again. Pasta is nothing but chicken soup when you leave out the soup. And the chicken. These days, everyone wants angel hair pasta in soup. If an old Jew eats it, it's called *chicken soup* and nobody cares. But call it *pasta in brodo* and throw in a little *Parmesan* and every hip young Jew in New York will order it in a second. Who cares if they're paying fourteen dollars for a twenty-cent bowl of soup?

Gefilte Fish (pronounced *geh-FILL-teh* fish). *Gefilte fish* is the quintessential Jewish dish. It was originated by Jews in Eastern Europe. Since they couldn't afford one whole fish, they gathered together pieces of leftover fish of different kinds, ground them up, added spices, patted them into shapes that were vaguely spherical and boiled them. The result was a new fish: *gefilte fish,* meaning "stuffed fish."

Gehakteh Leber (pronounced *geh-HAK-teh LEE-ber*). The literal translation would put a gleam into Jeffrey Dahmer's eye. It is "hacked liver." It is the original name of that dark-brown velvet substance—and we are not talking about Vanessa Williams—that goes by the street name "chopped liver." To a Jew or in fact to any veteran New Yorker, it has a secondary meaning.

You see a beautiful girl, and your friend says, "What a stunning girl." You say, "So what did you think she was, chopped liver?"

"Chopped liver" is always used as an unflattering comparison. If a guy is standing in line in a bank and he sees somebody push ahead of him, right away he says, "Mister, where are you going? Don't you see me standing here? What am I, chopped liver?"

Countries are compared to chopped liver, women are compared to chopped liver, shirts are compared to chopped liver. Real chopped liver, however, is only compared to other chopped liver. "You think this is good chopped liver? You should try my mother's."

SPANISH

There are only fourteen people in New York who are really Spanish from Spain, and they all work at Elaine's. The rest are Puerto Ricans, Dominicans, or Colombians, even though they may say they are Spanish, or they come from Cuba or from Uruguay or an obscure island in some archipelago that once belonged to Spain. Puerto Ricans, Dominicans, and Colombians love and are rightfully proud of their ancestral countries . . . at least when they speak to other Puerto Ricans, Dominicans, and Colombians. When they speak to anybody else, they suddenly become Cuban plantation owners who were forced to leave Cuba because they were the leaders of assassination plots against Castro while working as secret CIA agents, or they were Argentinean cowboys who fled the country after their affairs with Evita Peron were discovered.

We love listening to the local Spanish language radio station in New York, even though the only two words we understand in the course of a day's listening are, "abortion clinic." The language dances and sings, and our feet start moving to its rhythms when we hear it, but direct translations of some key phrases are less than romantic.

Chinga tu madre (polite translation). "Have intercourse with your mother."

Tu madre es un puta. "Your mother is a whore."
Be particularly attentive to any sentence directed at you containing the phrase "*su madre*." Usually the speaker is *not* complimenting your mother's cooking.

Of course, there is the ever-increasing notice in New York, *No habla inglés*. And if the response is "*No habla español*," this pretty much ensures that the conversation will be limited to a dance or a mugging.

ITALIAN

Few Italian words have become part of the survival vocabulary of New York. Italians tend to learn and adopt English as soon as possible. Since our polls reveal four out of seven Jewish wives have Italian lovers who take them to motels in New Jersey, the Italian men quickly realized that unless they wanted to keep striking out with the other three Jewish women who were holding out for Venezuelan oil millionaires, they'd better learn the language.

Italian, unlike the Spanish of the Puerto Rican, may sound strident and forceful, but it is usually rather gentle in context. Mainly it concerns food—and the ability to order four hundred different kinds of pasta. A healthy Italian man would rather have pasta than hang out with one of the four Jewish women in the New Jersey motel.

Index

Jackie Mason is a Tony Award–winning actor, comedian, author, and playwright who has written and starred in four hit Broadway one-man shows. His fifth, *Much Ado About Everything,* will open in 1998. **Raoul Felder** is an internationally famous divorce attorney to the stars. Together they have written one previous book, *Jackie Mason and Raoul Felder's Guide to New York & Los Angeles Restarurants,* and currently they are co-hosts of a new talk show on national public television, "Crossing the Line."

Illustrator **Sean DeLonas'** cartoons appear daily in the *New York Post.*